COUNT ME IN

COUNT ME

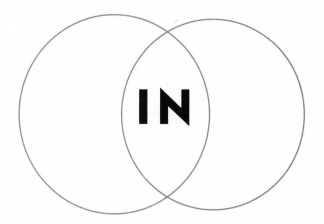

IN

How I stepped off the sidelines,
created connection, and
built a fuller, richer, more lived-in life

EMILY WHITE

McClelland & Stewart

Emily White would like to sincerely thank the Canada Council for the Arts, the Ontario Arts Council, and the Access Copyright Foundation for their generous support of this work.

Names and identifying characteristics of individuals discussed in this book have been changed to protect their privacy.

LIBRARY AND ARCHIVES CANADA CATALOGUING IN PUBLICATION

White, Emily J., 1970-, author
    Count me in : how I stepped off the sidelines, created connection, and built a fuller, richer, more lived-in life / Emily White.

Issued in print and electronic formats.
ISBN 978-0-7710-8771-4 (bound).--ISBN 978-0-7710-8774-5 (html)

1. Interpersonal relations. 2. Social interaction. 3. Relationship quality. 4. White, Emily Jane, 1970-. I. Title.

HM1106.W45 2015   302   C2014-904653-7
                                        C2014-904654-5

Psychological Home Scale (p. 278) © Sandra Sigmon, Stacy Whitcomb, and C.R. Snyder. Used with permission.

Neighbourhood Sense of Community Scale (p. 279) © Jack Nasar and David Julian. Used with permission.

Fear of Criticism Scale (p. 281) © Peter Bieling, Aaron Beck, and Gregory Brown. Used with permission.

Designed by Leah Springate
Typeset in Janson by Erin Cooper
Printed and bound in USA

McClelland & Stewart,
a division of Random House of Canada Limited,
a Penguin Random House Company
www.penguinrandomhouse.ca

1   2   3   4   5   19   18   17   16   15

Penguin
Random
House

For my family,
with thanks

We find ourselves not independently of other people and institutions but through them. We never get to the bottom of ourselves on our own.

—ROBERT BELLAH,
Habits of the Heart

CONTENTS

The Challenge of Belonging

Snakes, Stones, and a Recovery Plan

THE SUMMER OF 2012 wasn't a particularly great season for me. The previous year had been stressful: a long-term relationship had ended, and after some difficult weighing of my options, I'd left the coastal town I'd come to love and returned to the big inland city where I'd grown up and lived for much of my life. In the course of this big life change, I lost several friends, three pets, my house, and the plot of the book I'd been working on.

I wasn't very happy, but that didn't bother me too much, mostly because happiness has never been a primary interest of mine. In my first year of college, I scrawled out a quote from George Bernard Shaw that read, "Happiness and beauty are by-products." The statement felt true at the time, even if, at eighteen, I couldn't quite say why. Now, at forty-four, I understand it quite well. For me, happiness is and always has been a by-product of connection. I love feeling like there's a current running between me and the people around me, like I'm on the same wavelength as the places I'm in.

The line leading from connection to happiness was switched on early. From the age of four, I shared a bedroom with one of the happiest people on earth: the younger of my two older sisters, Terri. Terri seemed to have been born happy. It wasn't just that she was optimistic and had loads of energy for cheering others up. She *looked* happy: she had magical white-gold hair that caught the light and made it seem like she was moving within her own private sunbeam. And just as butterflies love sunshine, people flocked to Terri. My mother had a special phone line installed for all the calls coming in from friends and would-be boyfriends. As a little girl, I'd lie in bed and pretend to sleep while Terri talked non-stop. It was like listening to water breaking and falling over rocks.

That's what I came to value: not happiness itself – which I saw as something that people like Terri were naturally good at all on their own – but the sense of connection that came from lying in the dark and listening to the voice of someone I deeply loved. As I got older, I came to see that finding happiness through connection was really a better fit for my personality. It tied in with my natural desire to tinker, to break my moods down to their component parts and shuffle and reshape them until they were more to my liking. There was something hands-on about connection that appealed to me. If the feeling was a current, I could try to figure out what was blocking it, or assess why the flow felt just right.

Which was what I'd been doing in the small town I'd been living in. The book I lost when my life hit a bump had been about community. Something about the town had made community feel easy, and I'd been trying to zero in on what this was when I was told to pack my bags. The book became impossible – I couldn't write about small-town life in a city of five million people – but the research I'd done was still in my head, and I was puzzling over some of it that summer.

I knew, for instance, that the link I felt between connection and happiness held true for a lot of people. The Harvard University political scientist Robert Putnam argues that the single biggest predictor of happiness is the depth and breadth of your connections; that is, the more people you know, both socially and intimately, the happier you'll be.

That's what I couldn't sort out about my life in Toronto. My usual connection-to-happiness pathway didn't feel charged, and I couldn't spot the problem with the wiring, since I actually had more social ties in Toronto than in the small town I'd left. In fact, statistically, I had more ties than most people. The number of people we can count on has fallen in the past thirty years, even with the improvements we've seen in communication technology. On average, the most highly connected person now, complete with a smartphone and a Facebook page, has one-third fewer friends than her analogue counterpart did in 1985. No one can properly explain why this has happened. Some researchers say it's due to the isolating effects of technology; others say technology has saved us from the isolating effects of unstable jobs, lower incomes, and higher divorce rates. I wasn't sure which camp I was in, but it didn't really matter, because whichever way I looked at it, I was beating the average when it came to what researchers call *confidants*. I had four close friends whom I'd known for decades, as well as family members – my sisters Terri and Chris, my mother, my stepmother, and a bevy of nephews and nieces – who had mostly been in place my whole life. Furthermore, with the exception of one friend who'd moved from Toronto to rural Quebec, all my close ties lived in the same city as me.

Which meant that my sense of not being connected enough didn't really make sense. I'm fond of lists – they're essential if you're trying to analyze your own emotions – and that summer I started drawing up lists of people I knew, rating them as either "very close," "close," or "somewhat close." I spent some time deciding whether to shift Simon, the friend now in rural Quebec, from very close to close, but regardless, I wound up with eight names in the first two columns. I didn't have a "not close at all" column, because – although I had lots of former classmates in Toronto – acquaintances have really never occupied much space with me. I like seeing familiar faces on the subway and having catch-up conversations on sidewalks, but I rarely feel the need to rein someone from grade school back into my life. Which led me back to the problem that was nagging me: if acquaintances weren't the issue, and if I had loads of close ties, then why did I feel like some part of my emotional life was missing?

I was seeing a therapist that summer. As a recently separated, fortysomething female, doing so felt almost obligatory. And I didn't mind going, because I liked Genevieve. She was a grey-haired woman who filled her office with colourful cushions and bright, wall-sized tapestries. She seldom wore anything but black or beige, and I sometimes felt like all the colour was camouflage, meant to hide her as I focused on myself. It worked. The minute I stepped into her consulting room, I started on about the things that were bothering me – the separation, of course, which I hadn't chosen, but also the odd emptiness that had entered my life, the way I belonged to certain people in certain ways but had no *overall* sense of belonging.

"Can you remember a time when you did belong?" Genevieve asked, in her unobtrusive way.

I was about to describe life in my coastal town, but that sense of belonging was complicated by the fact that it had been taken away. Also, I was suddenly remembering something else.

"The Arctic," I said, and right away I could see it. I'd lived in the remote northern town of Iqaluit for six months in 2000 and had totally grooved on the place. It was insanely beautiful. Iqaluit sits north of the treeline, so if you're out on the land you can see for miles, and the remarkably colourful tundra is all heather and moss – gorgeous gold- and ruby-coloured surfaces so springy they make walking feel like bouncing on air.

"What made the Arctic special?" Genevieve asked. "Was it the people you knew?"

"Not really." My situation was a bit hard to explain. I'd been on contract with a law firm, but the contract was time-limited. This meant I hadn't formed strong friendships up north. I had met people and spent time with them, but since I'd known I wasn't staying, I hadn't tried to create close ties. Instead, I'd focused on the place itself. My roommate had a high-energy dog – half terrier, half husky – and after work Dakota and I would go for epic walks. It was summer, so the sun never set, and we'd hike hill after hill. Small herds of caribou would sometimes surround us. This was alarming at first, but I took my cues from Dakota and quickly learned the drill. The trick was to stand breathless and utterly still as the massive animals wound past, their eyes looking velvety in the white evening light. The caribou were so strange: I knew they could see me, but they glided by – sometimes only a half-foot away – as if I didn't exist. I was curious about them, and fascinated as well by the great stone statues that dotted the hills: the big inukshuks created by nomadic peoples to let others know they were not alone. I'd sometimes pose Dakota for photos at the base of these statues, telling her to "look northern." Often we'd just sit on boulders near the Labrador Sea and let the tide roll in around us.

In many ways, it was a difficult place: dirt roads that led nowhere, snippy arguments in cabs you had to share, and social lives that revolved around competitive games of crazy eights. The combination of boredom and lack of sleep did a lot of people in. I once arrived at work to find a colleague sitting at his desk and eating a procession of tiny doughnuts with the mechanical, blanked-out stare of someone officially gone.

But I was in my element. I had a black-lined sleeping bag that let me catch enough sleep; I had Dakota; and I had my lovely roommate, Rhonda, who placed the crazy eights trophy on top of our TV each time she won. (It was a Super Mario Pez dispenser.) The fact that I wasn't particularly close to anyone didn't matter, because I felt part of the place itself. My long walks were tying me to the land, to the animals, to the sea. I felt connected not to someone but to something, and that sense of connection grounded me and made me feel calmer and more secure than I usually had in my adult life.

"The funny thing," I told Genevieve, "is that sometimes I was probably in a whole lot of real danger. It was just me and Dakota out there on the hills. We could have gotten lost, or I could have turned an ankle." There had been one particularly bad moment when Dakota refused to climb a hill and I began to panic – alone in the middle of nowhere – that there was a polar bear on the other side. When Dakota turned and headed straight home, I followed. I never did learn what she was leading me away from, but the memory always left me with the throat-tightening sense of having been saved. However, I decided to gloss this over and emphasize what was mostly true. "I never felt unsafe there," I said.

"Do you feel unsafe here?" *Here* was Toronto, of course: the city I'd been raised in and knew as well as the inside of my palm.

I wasn't sure what to say. I felt physically safer in Toronto – it's a busy place, with lots of eyes and ears on the ground – but something was missing psychologically. It was as if gravity wasn't working properly. I wasn't rooted enough; sometimes my life just felt too light.

"There's none of those statues I used to see on the hills," I said, trying to explain. "I loved the message in them. People put all this work into creating symbols of togetherness. Like, even if they weren't together right then, they were together in spirit. They were thinking of each other."

"And is that how you feel? Like no one's thinking of you?"

"Well, maybe not enough people. Not people I don't know." This sounded strange even to me, but Genevieve seemed to get it.

"Your life's too small," she suggested.

"That's it." She'd come up with the phrase that had been eluding me. "Up north, everything felt big. I mean, it *was* big. The Arctic's a big place. But I felt bigger too. There was just more to me. And I feel like I don't have that anymore."

"Could you recreate it?"

"The Arctic?"

"The feeling you had up there."

"Well, Toronto is a pretty different place," I said. "And Dakota must be gone by now. It was a long time ago, and she was a big dog. She wouldn't be alive anymore."

I didn't like thinking of Dakota disappearing. It felt unfair. Much in the same way, I had to admit, that my own life was feeling mildly unfair, as if I were being shortchanged on something I couldn't fully name.

"The Arctic," I said, groping for a better explanation. "It wasn't just *people*."

"It was . . . what do you call it: 'the land'?"

It sounded funny coming from Genevieve, but she had it right. No one up north said "outside" or "nature." It was just the land – all around you and right up close. And the land had a mystical quality that made me feel as though I was never quite seeing all of it. The sky at midnight was a hazy, glossy white that made doors and walls look less like hard surfaces and more like objects you might reach through. It was as if other worlds were present, and very close by, and sometimes I'd lie in the yard with Dakota's head on my belly and think about how there was more on offer than I could ever take in.

I shook the memory off. Genevieve's office was on a main street, and traffic was thundering by. She had the air conditioning on, so the room was cool, but she couldn't do anything about the August sun. It was bouncing off the roads and buildings in a way that made me want to squint indoors.

"I can't recreate that here," I said.

"It seems to me you're talking about a feeling, not a place," she replied quietly. "You're talking about belonging to something bigger than you. Does that have to be the Arctic?"

I shook my head. No. Even I could see that setting the Arctic as the standard for belonging was setting the bar way too high. I knew there had to be other ways to recreate the feeling, ways that were accessible to me in my ordinary city and over the course of my day-to-day life. But I immediately ran into a problem that Genevieve didn't seem aware of.

"Other things are gone, you know." It was a point I'd taken from my community research: the ways in which we had previously connected were vanishing. Gone were the lifelong club memberships, the smoky union halls, the neighbourhood coffee klatches, the boisterous campaign meetings, the

friendly bowling leagues. The word that came up in the
research was *public* – we'd lost a good deal of public life and
had been left with lives that were strictly private. But we were
never designed for strictly private lives. For one thing, a life
composed of just friends and family members is a vulnerable
one: if anyone walks out, or gets relocated for work, your
social world shrinks. More importantly, private ties can't turn
us into all we need to be. Friends and family reinforce parts
of who we are – usually the parts we share with them – but we
need bigger and less personal worlds to reveal everything
we *might* be.

When Putnam wrote about the links between connection and happiness, he stressed both breadth and depth in
relationships. By this, he meant that we need close, intimate ties as well as steady ties that are broader and more
casual, that don't depend on deep conversation or intense
sharing. But he went on to say that these broader ties are
disappearing: today, there's less for us to belong to, less for
us to be part of as we try to shore up a thicker, less personal, more lively sense of inclusion.

Reading this made me uneasy, since I had a lot of experience with things disappearing. I used to be a lawyer, and
until the mid-aughts I practised environmental protection
law. This meant I protected things under threat, and the
threatened things that interested me the most were animals. I was an expert on creatures leaving this world. I
could rattle off the top ten mammals on the international
Red List of endangered species and picture the creepy dia-
gram that always accompanies such lists – the one that runs

with a thick dotted line from "vulnerable" to "threatened" to actually gone. It's a perverse mental tic of mine to fixate on what's on its way out. The future doesn't seem to interest me nearly as much as the past, especially a past with losses in it that promise to be irreversible. Whenever I look at species lists, the "extinct" category always fills me with dread. I'll read about passenger pigeons and try to understand how something so gorgeous could be allowed to slip by, how we could just eliminate something – those amazing, sky-filling flocks of birds – that gave us something we essentially need.

I wondered if a sense of belonging was nudging toward the "extinct" category. Research from the University of Oregon has shown that the number of Americans who feel a sense of belonging has fallen by half from 1976 to today, and this applies to both genders as well as all ages and education levels. However, the numbers haven't hit bottom, which made me think that if I had to peg belonging to a column, I'd list it as threatened, not gone. So although it may be harder to find, it's still around if you know where to look.

The thought of looking for belonging appealed to me. It aligned with my tendency to fiddle, to fix an emotional hole by twisting my life upside down and sideways until I could spot where the air was leaking out. But I wasn't sure how this search would make me feel. If we were losing belonging, would looking for it feel like reading the endangered species lists for months on end? Would it leave me gasping for air in the same way the lists did, with each additional species feeling like another hand around my neck?

Other people probably don't need such reminders, but as I walked home from Genevieve's office that day, I had to tell myself that thinking and doing were two different things. Thinking about disappearing species was draining, but the one time I'd done something about it, I hadn't felt drained at all.

A lot of my work as a lawyer involved writing memos about things like species habitat. It was an office job; no one ever asked me to park myself in front of a bulldozer. But then I was hired by a magazine to write about a highly endangered snake. The snake was called the blue racer, and my task was to spend a week with a research crew searching for them on an island in Lake Erie.

I was a hopeless fieldworker. Everyone else seemed born for this sort of thing, or at least perfectly equipped: they had air mattresses, patched tents, and pocket knives; they knew how to create large meals out of canned goods and listen to hockey games at night without showing signs of boredom. They were patient with me – they understood they had to put up with me if they wanted the snake's photo in the magazine. This meant they didn't groan too loudly when I fell off logs, watched my boots sink in mud, or announced we all had to stop because I'd somehow lost my scarf.

In many ways, I was more curious about the field-workers than I was about the snakes. The snakes weren't around. That's what "highly endangered" meant: that you could walk for days without seeing one. The fieldworkers, on the other hand, were always close by, since they wouldn't let me walk the snake lines alone. I had plenty of time to wonder about their psychology. They were all grad students, and they knew all the facts: there were only three hundred blue racers left in the world, all of which were on that island, and every one of them was under threat from an expanding quarry. But this dismal scenario didn't seem to affect their mood. The fieldworkers were an energetic bunch, brewing coffee on their windmill-powered stove and drinking water from old Nalgene bottles they never bothered to wash. To me, it was a mystery: how could they maintain high spirits in the midst of what might be a futile effort?

The question was answered for me one afternoon when the lead biologist, Ben, came out of the woods with a blue racer wrapped around his arm.

"Do you want to hold it?" he asked. Ben was tall and spectacled and looked exactly like an embattled conservationist from a movie: hair unbrushed and eyes intense, with an unnerving way of freezing mid-stride the instant he spotted a snake.

"I'd love to hold it," I replied. I held my hands out like someone expecting a Christmas present. Ben grabbed my hands in a way people don't usually do at Christmas – he shoved them closer together – and then, after assuring himself I wasn't going to drop it, he let the snake slither from his hand to mine.

I was transported. The snake's skin felt cool and surprisingly dry as it wound its way up my arm, and it was so beautiful, with shimmering streaks of blue down its silvery sides. Its eyes, when it turned to look at me, were a soft brown, and its expression was uncanny: all-knowing and almost forgiving.

Then I got it. That was what kept the biologists going. The creature they were trying to save was marvellous, and throwing themselves into saving it – even if it meant finishing every day covered with cuts and torn clothing – felt better than doing nothing. There was actually less pain, and a lot more fun, in tackling something head-on instead of letting it go.

About halfway home from Genevieve's office, I stopped near a dog park to relive that moment in the woods – the way the world had cracked open and I'd felt let in on the secret of just how wonderful a simple creature could be. I knew that this was the memory that would have to guide me if I was going to look for belonging. And I suddenly realized I *was* going to look for belonging. It was the ultimate emotional fix-it project, something I could throw myself into and up against until my life felt as full as it had in the Arctic, until I was once again rooted and connected in ways that went beyond my own private ties. I even knew how to frame what I was looking for. The more highly endangered an animal is, the more likely there is to be a "recovery plan" in place for it – some strategy meant to revive it or keep it from slipping any further toward the ranks of "gone." That's what I needed for belonging. I wanted a specific and practical plan that would help me restore a larger, more public sense of connection and make it a reality in the here and now.

The question was where to start. Most recovery plans begin by asking what's essential to the species' survival, and the only word that was coming to me when I thought of belonging was *dog*. I missed Dakota, and right then I was staring at a couple of dogs queuing in very human fashion for a ground-level fountain that owners operated with their feet.

I wondered if I should be aiming a bit higher. Maybe inclusion in some great club would be a good starting point. Then I realized that all the clubs I could think of were men-only – the Shriners, the Knights of Columbus – and when I struggled to recall their female equivalents, my mind went blank. I couldn't quite picture this sort of belonging. The last time I'd seen a Shriners' parade was in 1989; the men had been wearing fez hats and driving tiny cars. I doubted the Shriners still did this, but then I realized I didn't know what it was they *did* do. Thinking about belonging in this way doesn't come naturally anymore – not just to me, but probably not to anyone born after 1960 or even earlier. It was clear that I had to belong in modern ways, ways that weren't likely going to involve meeting halls, pledges, or the wearing of boxy caps.

Which brought me back to *dog*. I wasn't sure what I meant by this, but I decided not to question it. It was answer enough to the question Genevieve had posed: when had I found a sense of belonging in the past? The question struck me as important at the time, and I've come to realize that it's absolutely critical. Even with belongingness rates in free fall, most of us still know what we need to feel glued in. We've all had experiences with feeling right at the centre of things, and even if those experiences have ended, they can serve as a guide to where we might find belonging in the future.

I sat on a bench to think. For me, *dog* was a clue to what I needed; it was some reference to the past that was pointing me forward. I looked at the small park in front of me – a baseball diamond, picnic tables, grass, and the shade cast by old maples – and thought *nature*. It certainly wasn't the Arctic, but it was a space that felt meaningful to me – vastly more meaningful than the busy street I'd just come from. The natural world seemed like a blessing, and I remembered a time in my life when people talked about blessing in a literal way, as an aspect of belief. I liked the way these memories made me feel – I remembered the scratchy feel of the kilt I used to wear to convent school – and decided to add *faith* to the list. Then there was Terri, and the cramped bedroom we used to share, with clothes all over the floor and her under the covers with the phone to her ear, and I thought of *home* and *neighbourhood*. Those words came with some underpinning of alarm, of something having gone wrong, but I didn't want to think about that right then, so I just kept the words on my mental list and pushed the feelings aside.

I understood that my list might grow, but at least I had some starting points, and they all came from a deeply personal place. Later, once I'd begun the challenge, I was surprised at how quickly I lost sight of my list and let others tell me what I needed for belonging, but I found that thinking back to that very first list steered me back on course. Having real, almost spontaneous, starting points is crucial, because one thing I've learned over the course of this challenge is that if you're not honest with yourself about what you need for belonging, you likely will not find it. Certain activities might be interesting – like volunteering at a food bank – but if that activity isn't meaningful to you, it won't lead to the sense of inclusion you're looking for.

Dog, nature, faith, home, neighbourhood. The list felt a bit garbled, like clues to a mystery I'd have to tease out. But at least I had the clues. They were like the tracts of land or specific food sources that get listed in recovery plans. They didn't fit together as neatly as I might have liked, but I recognized them as the essentials of what I would come to define as my belongingness challenge. They were where I had to start.

Looking back to that moment in the park, I'm surprised at how right I was about one thing. At no point in my year and a half of looking for belonging did I even stumble upon an opportunity to join the sorts of large groups that seem to have been ubiquitous in the past. I did manage to join, or rejoin, the Catholic Church, and the Vatican certainly counts as a large organization, but the specific group I joined had fewer than thirty members. Aside from faith organizations, large groups simply didn't surface. It's not that I was avoiding them. They weren't there.

Without setting out to do so, I wound up confirming a major point in the research on belonging: the groups you'll find will probably be small and informally structured. The connection that these groups offer is sometimes described as "loose," meaning it doesn't flow from organizations with hierarchies or long histories. Loose connections are often held up as inferior to the sorts of lifelong ties that people used to bring to clubs like the Woodmen of the World, but – having never been a Woodman – I can't make that judgment.

I can say that many of the ties I found didn't feel all that loose. It's true that there was more flexibility to the groups, and more coming and going of members, but this informality might have made my search for belonging easier. In fact, over the course of this challenge, I hit on a sort of sub-rule: the more formality there is attaching to a group – application forms, orientation sessions, training guides – the less belonging that group will probably offer. This isn't because there's anything wrong with formality itself, but rather because the formality is often a sign that the group is looking for a certain type of person. If you're not that person – if you are not, say, eager to walk alone at dawn collecting injured songbirds (and I did this) – you're less likely to find a sense of fit there.

I also learned that the emphasis on the size or structure of groups themselves is a bit misplaced. It's true that some groups just get belonging wrong from the start. A lot depends, for instance, on the skills of the group leader. In the course of one project – which involved standing nose-to-snout with hogs – I felt a sense of belonging right away. This wasn't because of anything I was doing, but because the woman leading the group was a connection genius: she knew how to weave people together, how to welcome newbies, and how to make people feel, even if they'd only shown up two or three times, like they'd been around for ages. Beth wasn't trying to make anyone feel like they belonged. She was just a deeply kind person who extended kindness to everyone she met, meaning the group was filled with relaxed, reassured people who were generally pretty nice to each other. In other situations, I've watched group leaders box belonging out. When I tried to become an evangelical Christian, for instance, the group leader was so nervous and apprehensive that she made everyone in the group feel nervous and apprehensive as well.

For a while, I thought that group leadership skills were the key to belonging – that it was the leaders who were creating the sense of connection. In a sense, they were, but what they were really doing was modelling certain behaviours and attitudes I had to learn myself. I've come to think that the number one block to belonging today might not be busy schedules, long commutes, or even overt acts of rejection, but just not *knowing* enough about how to belong. I'm not sure that belonging is in the same league as riding a bike. If you've been cut off for a while, or overworked for too long, or just not paying attention, you can lose some of the skills it requires. These aren't hard skills, like knowing how to operate a circular saw, but they're skills nonetheless: how to trust, how to cooperate, how to expect certain outcomes and not expect others. I know that the main thing I had to do, right at the start of this challenge, was identify why I felt a bit *cagey* around belonging. The answer I hit on surprised me – and involved me standing in the middle of a massive condo development – but it made me realize that I was bringing the wrong ideas to belonging, and that I'd have to change these in order to successfully connect to others.

I don't want to make belonging sound like some solo project that's entirely about you. It's not. In fact, the very best thing about belonging is that, as soon as you start looking for it, you realize there are a lot of other people looking too. You do have to take the first few steps alone. You have to get to the meeting, to the garden, to the neighbourhood cleanup. And you might feel alone heading out the door, but once you arrive, you lose your sense of aloneness. In fact, in arriving you end up doing double duty, because you help someone else lose *their* sense of aloneness. After all, we never connect in isolation. We always connect to others. Which means that when we go looking for togetherness, we conjure it up.

ONE

Hagerty's Rule

What You Need for Belonging

EVEN THOUGH I HAD my starting points, I was surprised at how ready others were to tell me where to start – and how ready I was to listen. A few weeks after my dog park revelation, while having dinner with two friends who'd made the "very close" column in my relationship list, I mentioned that I was going to look for more connection. I didn't describe it as an overall challenge or fundamental goal. I just said that, being back in Toronto, I wanted to "flesh things out a bit."

There's nothing unusual about saying this. Belonging's quite fashionable. We have no trouble with sites like LinkedIn or Meetup that claim to facilitate a greater sense of connection. The technology is new, of course, but so is the promise of easy access to connection. I tend to be overly nostalgic about the past – mostly because there were more animals in it – and my dad often tried to warn me away from this, saying that his past had been pretty heavy on things like poverty and pretty light on things like food. Still, despite the deprivation he confronted in other areas, his past was full of *people*. He was born in a small Kentucky town in 1928, and he spent his first eighteen years surrounded by kin, neighbours, and fellow faith members. In the letter that he wrote to my sisters and me the year before he died, the pages are just crammed with people who were a daily part of each other's lives: my fiddle-playing great-uncles, my father's doting grandparents, the parish priest who would host festivals that saw chickens appearing in cages and disappearing as meals. My dad didn't live to see the era of Meetup or Facebook, but I think he would have found the notion of people searching for connection online a bit futuristic.

It didn't strike my friends Juliette and Andrew as futuristic. We *were* the future. More specifically, we were part of what's been called the "post-civic" generation – that is, the generation that's grown up without much in the way of a larger, more public social life. The two of them took no offence, as we sat in their back garden, to me saying that I needed more than they could offer. They understood. We'd all known each other for decades: Juliette and I had gone to high school together, and Andrew and I had been college roommates. When they married in 2010, it was like having my private life sharpened. Two people I knew extremely well were now together, meaning that conversations sometimes felt like flipping through my own diaries – we knew the same people, had gone to the same schools, and spoke with the same sad nostalgia about the death of Kurt Cobain. They'd been stalwarts after my separation: we were having dinner that night because Juliette, during my first week back, had taken one look at my haggard face and said she'd like to cook for me. That first dinner had been ritualized, with no discussion and no fanfare, into a meal every week. When I tried, a few months in, to thank her for this, she waved a dishtowel at me and said, "Shut up. We love you."

Part of loving me was steering me toward the bigger life they agreed that I needed. As soon as I said "connection," Andrew hit on a plan. In college, he'd been skinny and underfed, lost in layers of T-shirts and hair that fell half-way down his back. At forty-one, he was toned, focused, and crew-cut, and he attributed some of this change to yoga. He was a devotee – the kind of guy who could hold a plank pose for ages – and he was amazed I hadn't already tried the studio a few blocks from my apartment.

"You have one of the best studios in town near you," he said. "Possibly the best in the country. And it's so *close* to you."

He travelled forty-five minutes each morning to get there. The fact that I lived within walking distance but hadn't yet put in an appearance struck him as borderline criminal.

"You *really* need to try it," he said. It was still warm enough for us to be eating outside, and I tossed my napkin onto the wicker table and tipped my head back. Their yard was one of my favourite spots in town: mysteriously silent, with the branches of an oak tree overhanging the garden, and pots of basil and mint lining the steps to the door. It was a mystery to me why anyone would want to leave such a place, but Andrew was adamant that the benefits of the practice outweighed the hassles of the commute.

"There's something very grounding about yoga. I think you could really use that now. It's peaceful, and it helps with your breathing, and—"

"I'll go!" I said, trying to appease him.

I didn't mention that yoga was already on my list of alternate connection possibilities. When I listened to what women my age were doing for togetherness, there was a lot of talk about Pilates, meditation retreats, distance running, and strange new crossbreeds like Tough Mudder contests. There seemed to be an awful lot of emphasis on endurance – going for days without talking, immersing yourself in a full-body ice bath. I wasn't sure what all the endurance training was actually leading to, but as someone high in stamina and moderately skilled in contemplation, I decided a yoga class was doable.

I sought out the studio's schedule online and presented myself for a beginners' class. The woman who took my money looked angelic – with a soft halo of blonde hair around a supremely calm face – and when I admitted to being a bit nervous, she replied that it wasn't unusual.

"I'll take you into the room myself," she said. The studio was divided in two. The front room, where we were talking, had low padded benches, a large desk, and two unobtrusive racks of clothing for sale. The light in this room was stark, streaming in through high-set windows and bouncing off the walls in a way that made the space almost uncomfortably bright. Beyond the front area, I could see the edge of a slightly darker room: here, someone must have pulled the blinds, because the light was muted and honey coloured. The floors were buffed and gleaming, and they seemed to be absorbing light instead of reflecting it. *If I lie down on that*, I thought, staring at the floor with a certain degree of longing, *it will be like lying on a tanning bed.*

I was thinking happy thoughts about heated floors when my guide blocked the door.

"It's a shoe-free zone," she said, pointing to my runners. Then she gestured toward a tall shelving unit. "You can put them there," she added. There was a chair beside the shelves. This was clearly where people stopped to strip off their footwear, but I froze.

I have what might be called issues with my feet. "You get those from your father," my mother once said, glancing at my feet and making it sound like my dad had come along and sewn them on after I was born. They're heavily callused, and the calluses are so thick they split open at the sides and heels. The skin is dry, and no matter how much moisturizer I slather on, it has a creepy tendency to flake. Worst of all, my baby toes slide under each foot instead of extending straight out. When we were young, Terri used to try to twist these toes back into position, a bit of chiropractic that always left me squirming as she explained, "I'm just trying to make you *normal*."

Terri never hurt me all that much, but I carry some mild psychic scars. It's almost impossible for me to show my feet to anyone – especially not a stranger whose own feet looked so dewy and unblemished that they were almost baby-like.

"Can I do it in my socks?" I asked.

The clerk looked puzzled. "No. You won't get the grip you need, and that can be dangerous. You have to be able to anchor yourself to the mat."

There was no escaping the situation. With all the enthusiasm of a suspect settling in for a cross-examination, I sat down and removed my footwear. I was expecting a startled "Gross!" but the clerk looked away from my feet, an act of avoidance that made me feel more, not less, self-conscious.

"You can just stretch out," she said, perhaps a bit more coolly than before, as we entered the studio. I was right: the floors were toasty. People were lying flat on their backs, not talking to each other, in various spots around the room. Most had their eyes closed.

I spread out my mat and lay down like everyone else. This was immediately soothing. One thing we're a bit short on, culturally, is time spent with others for no reason. If we're together, we increasingly need to make something of that time, by talking, shopping, or going to the movies. Sociologists describe this sort of behaviour as "active socializing" – meaning that we're out and about, doing stuff. The opposite is "passive socializing," which basically translates into reading the paper while your spouse fusses over something on the stove. Over the past two decades, sociologists have been watching passive socializing fall and active socializing rise. It's the inevitable result of more people living solo: if you're home alone and want to see someone, you usually have to set a date to *do* something. There's nothing wrong with this, but it does mean we have fewer moments of just being with others quietly. And nothing is a nice thing to do. As I lay on the ground before the yoga class started and listened to the people around me breathe, I felt the reassurance that comes with being part of a group and not having to prove yourself in any way.

That feeling began to slip when the class began. I liked the instructor, who introduced himself as Derek, right away, partly because he wasn't wearing yoga clothes – just a loose tank top and a pair of what looked like beach shorts. His slight shabbiness was appealing. Even though Derek was six feet tall and so solid he might as well have been made of wood, his clothes gave him the air of someone baggier and not too intense. When he spoke, his voice had the same effect: everything he said sounded exactly like the last thing he'd said. He was taking us through poses – *chest open, downward dog, upward dog, hips to the wall, weight on your heels* – but his intonation was so even that it was like listening to someone murmur in his sleep. I had very little idea of what Derek was talking about; he gave little indication of registering what he was saying, and the overall effect was less like a workout and more like storytime in the library.

Or at least it felt that way to me. For a lot of the moves, especially if I was in downward dog, my hair flipped over my headscarf in a way that blocked my view of the room. It was only when I was upright that I could see how hard the others were working. I couldn't begin to keep up, but I wasn't troubled by this. Even though the other practitioners were very good, they didn't seem competitive. I did get the sense that they were having an emotional experience that was escaping me – their eyes were sharply focused, like they were searching out something in the distance – but whatever it was they were glimpsing remained out of sight for me. My own concerns remained pretty mundane. Sweat was trickling both up and down my face, and I was trying to keep my balance as lifelong problems with low blood pressure made the transitions from bending to standing feel like dips on a roller coaster ride.

It was a relief when Derek told us to sit. But I was astonished when he told us what to do while sitting. We were to cross our legs and then, with our palms flat to the mat, lift our entire bodies up with our hands. For me, this was fantasy. I could barely cross my legs. And the position had the unfortunate effect of casting my feet into view: there they were, jutting out in front of me, one sad specimen crossed over the other like chunks of meat in a butcher shop. To my horror, Derek – who until that point had not paid me much attention – came over and crouched in front of me.

"You can do this," he said in his cat-like voice.

"Actually, I can't."

"You can. I want you to feel what it's like." And even as I was trying to disagree, he took my feet in his hands and lifted me up. My entire body came off the mat. I felt suddenly weightless, or, more precisely, so expertly supported that my weight no longer mattered. The levity shot from my body to my mind. Derek was very close to me, his loose clothes and crouched posture making him look like a beggar from some medieval painting, and I was staring at him, wide-eyed. The sexual overtones of what was happening weren't lost on me so much as totally irrelevant. A stranger was holding my weight in his hands, and the pulse of connection that flowed from his grip was so strong it felt nearly electric.

"There," Derek said, after a few blurry moments. He was letting me go. I was still staring at him. My bottom slowly sank. He smiled, and went back to circling the room.

"Corpse pose," he said, and I lay back in a state of near bliss. For the first time since the class had begun, I felt in sync with the others, deeply relaxed, and mildly high. Derek's hands – the selflessness he'd displayed in holding my awful feet – had moved me to the core. The touch felt like a ritual; it ushered me into the larger group. I felt part of the room itself, almost one with the wooden floor, and also part of the collective that had found transformation under the guidance of this amazing teacher.

There was no formal shift out of this relaxed state, no chanting or ringing of a bell. Derek just started talking like a normal person, using a louder, more ordinary voice to say ordinary things.

"Great effort today," he said, sounding like someone you'd hear in a cafeteria. "If you have questions, just come to the front."

I had no questions. I was still dazed, but I felt I had this connection thing licked. Finding it had been so easy, and so sensual. I donned my shoes without concern and floated out of the studio into what was now early evening. The late September sky was that in-between shade I love – not blue nor black, but purple – and the heady light made the street seem magical. There was a fruit and flower stand across the

road, and as I sailed in the door in search of oranges, I recognized a woman from the class. I gave a her a big, toothy
smile – the sort of smile I might give Juliette, or Terri, or
anyone else I felt particularly close to. But instead of smiling, this woman did something strange. She looked right at
me and turned away.

My sense of connection crashed. It was like having my
clothes stripped off. I felt so exposed and embarrassed that
I almost reached to cover myself. I was already flushed
from the class, but I could feel a different sort of colour
creeping up around my neck; pretty soon my whole face
was going to be bright red. I didn't want anyone to see this,
but I didn't know where to go. The shop was small – just
three aisles wide – and I didn't know which aisle the woman
was about to go down. I couldn't avoid her, but I couldn't
face that look again. So I did something which in other
circumstances might have been comical: I backed out the
door without turning around, like someone being ordered
away at gunpoint.

I stopped on the sidewalk in the cool evening air and
tried to catch my breath. Even though she was the one at
fault, I felt *I* was the one who'd made a mistake. I started
rifling through what this might be. Should I not have
smiled? Not have assumed some sort of fellow feeling? I
started to walk – I always walk when I'm anxious – but no
matter how fast I moved, I couldn't shake what felt like a
slap of rejection.

This in itself was a bit surprising. Not the sense of rejection, but my inability to shake it. Even if I feel rejection

intensely, it usually wears off fairly quickly. There's a reason for this. In 2004, the UCLA neurologist Naomi Eisenberger showed that social pain and physical pain overlap in our heads. When Eisenberger used an MRI scanner to examine the brains of students who'd just been socially rejected, she found that the neural circuits involved in physical pain were lit up. In a follow-up experiment, she had some students stare at a photo of someone who'd just broken up with them, while other students were given painful heat stimulations. Again, the same neural regions were activated, regardless of whether the pain was emotional or physical.

There are some surprising aspects to what's now referred to as the social pain/physical pain overlap. For instance, it's been found that Tylenol, which relieves physical pain, can also act as a buffer against social pain. Moreover, it's been shown that sensitivity to pain in one area can act as a predictor in the other: if you feel physical pain fast and acutely, you'll likely get hit hard with emotional pain as well.

In this respect, I was lucky, since I'd been born with a high pain threshold. On one of my first bike trips after getting back from the coast, I fell not off but *onto* my bike. It was like being turned into a cubist painting: part of me was caught above the handlebars, another part was near the gearshift, and everything from my shoulder to my hip was suspended on the frame while my legs lay on the ground. It hurt like hell. But after ten minutes of sitting on the park steps and pulling myself together, I thought, *Well, I'm here.* And then I sped off for an hour of cycling, the pain more or less forgotten.

All the women in my family are like this. My mom had three kids without anaesthetic, and in their early teens – while our parents were getting divorced – Chris and Terri fought like Vikings. They were both big, and apparently indestructible. I once sat cross-legged beside the banister and watched Terri push Chris halfway down a flight of stairs. There was a startled moment as Terri and I both held our breath – then Chris hit the landing, stood, and tore right back up after Terri. (They were always careful, since I was so little, to pause in their fighting and sidestep me.)

Overall, we're a sturdy bunch; we would have made good frontier wives. I sometimes think our physical ruggedness is wasted on modernity – there's no need for us to be hauling logs or hacking through icy streams – but it's left us well equipped to deal with the modern threat of rejection. After Chris had outgrown her Norse invader phase and turned into a calm, intensely beautiful young woman, she registered for a computer science degree and realized that she'd be the only female in the class. This was the early eighties, when only guys with a love of punch cards signed up for programming. "They'll be assholes," she said meditatively, and then spent the next four years getting mildly razzed while only mildly caring.

The problem with the rejection in the store was that I couldn't sort it out. My high pain threshold couldn't help, because the pain was unfocused. Experts stress that it's "ambiguous" rejection that does the most damage when we're looking for belonging. If someone tells you, "You're not welcome here, and this is the reason why," it's like falling off your bike. You can attend to the pain and move on. But if there's no reason, it's like being pinned to the ground. You can't get up because you don't know what knocked you down in the first place.

I tried to not let this stop me. There was so much I liked about the studio – the friendly desk clerk (who eventually introduced herself as Shelley), the gorgeous floors, Derek's amazing hands. But each time I went, I felt the residue of that woman's rejection. And in trying to explain it, I wound up making it worse, because I became fixated on all the differences between me and the other class members: I was wearing baggy track pants while they were in fitted yoga gear; I had my Mennonite-type headscarf while others had elastic hair bands; I tipped over during the sun salutation while they kept their balance; and so on.

The more differences I noticed, the more cut off I began to feel. The original rejection was acting like a virus, spreading out to taint my whole experience. This mattered. Research on belonging as a field in its own right – as opposed to just as an offshoot of friendship or social support – began in 1995, with the publication of a major paper by Roy Baumeister, then at Case Western Reserve University, and Mark Leary, then at Wake Forest University. I sometimes feel that every generation needs something obvious spelled out to it, and the whole point of Baumeister and Leary's paper was that we need to belong. The two psychologists put lack of belonging right up there with hunger and thirst. Their argument was that if we don't get enough belonging, bad things start to happen. Depression and anxiety skyrocket; stress becomes overwhelming; our health starts to fail; we lose the ability to problem-solve; and we become easy targets for jealousy, hostility, even early death. And with social pain and physical pain overlapping, we can start to *feel* unwell, often for reasons we might not be able to name.

The paper was a landmark in the field and is still frequently cited by other researchers in the areas of community and connection. But Baumeister and Leary had a slightly clumsy approach to belonging itself. They described it as the result of "frequent interaction plus persistent caring." They seemed to take it as a given that readers just knew what belonging was, and most probably did, but "just knowing" wasn't a strong enough basis for future research.

It was University of Michigan nursing professor Bonnie Hagerty, who was interested in the health-promoting effects of belonging, who provided a more workable definition. After polling students, hospital patients, and – for unexplained reasons – Catholic nuns about feelings of visibility, inclusion, and acceptance, Hagerty set out the following definition:

> Belonging = a sense of being welcomed, needed, or accepted by a group + a sense of fitting or matching with that group.

The key thing about Hagerty's definition – which I found so workable that I came to think of it as Hagerty's Rule – is that *both* elements have to be in place. If the fit is wrong, or if the fit is right but you feel unwelcome, belonging will remain out of reach.

What the woman in the fruit store did was break the first leg of Hagerty's Rule. She made me feel unwelcome. Her cold glance suggested something wasn't quite right about me, that I might not belong in the way I thought I belonged. I have to stress that, in all my months of looking for belonging, I didn't really have this experience again. I did confront rejection once more, but in a sense it was an easier sort of rejection to deal with, since it was literally spelled out for me. There was nothing ambiguous about it, and the lack of ambiguity meant I could decide on how to respond.

At the yoga studio, I was still confused, still unsure of myself. I might have been able to tough it out if it weren't for the fact of the rate card. My cheap two-week pass had expired, and I needed to know how much classes actually cost.

"It's a little confusing," Shelley said, handing me the card. "It depends on how much you pay up front and how often you attend."

Math has never been one of my strong suits, but even a quick glance at the card told me the numbers I was seeing were oversized.

"You get the most value if you pay for a year," Shelley was saying, but I was no longer listening. All the options were out of my price range. This shouldn't have felt like another rejection, but it did. The card was telling me I could only belong if my income was above a certain point, and this was something my high pain threshold couldn't really assist with. Social pain is linked to physical pain, but it can also be linked to your bank account, and if the social pain arises because you can't afford to belong, taking a Tylenol won't change a thing.

This is an unnerving situation to find yourself in. The Oregon study that found lowered rates of belonging among Americans had one exception: the rich. The link between affluence and belonging has been noted for decades. As early as the 1970s, the sociologist Reed Larson warned of companionship becoming a "luxury good," one more readily available to the well-heeled and less available to everyone else.

It's not that the wealthy are better at connection. Rather, as we've lost free time, steady jobs, lifelong marriages, and the bevy of social clubs that used to exist, connection has been commodified into something we can buy. I ultimately became so interested in the relationship between buying and belonging that I decided to create a whole project around it. My results were mixed, but I did manage to find belonging in this way. To think you can't buy it today is a mistake; you can. But Arlie Russell Hochschild, a sociologist at the University of California, Berkeley, has been sounding the alarm bell on this for years, arguing that if we rely on the market, we forget how to connect in non-market ways. I found the prospect of forgetting so disturbing that I decided everything else I did in this challenge – with the exception of my "buying" project – would be done for free.

"I'll have to check on this," I said breezily, as if a thousand-dollar tab was no problem.

Shelley – who couldn't have been earning much herself – was looking at me with a slight air of apology. She said she looked forward to seeing me again.

Still feeling disconcerted, both by the discussion of money and by my overall lack of it, I stopped at the bottom of the stairwell to pull myself together. There was a notice board near the doorway covered with posters for yoga DVDs, meditation retreats, organic food delivery, and then, somewhat surprisingly, a flyer about a Jack Russell rescue group. I took one look at the photo – a little dog with enormous eyes wearing a cheerful red vest – and instantly tore the tag off the bottom.

There was something hugely appealing about animals right then. Although I didn't notice it for a few moments, I realized I was back to my original starting point: the word *dog*.

I think there's a risk of overanalyzing your own motivations, but over the course of this challenge, I did have to wonder about the role animals were playing. They came up constantly, appearing in my projects on home, neighbourhood, caring, and volunteering. If it weren't for the fact that only guide dogs are allowed in church, they probably would have surfaced in my faith project as well. It's not just that I *like* animals; it's that they seem crucial to me. And this is probably because I've never seen much of a difference between connecting to animals and connecting to people.

Part of this attitude, like my high pain threshold, was probably inherited, or at least taught. My mother was the sort of woman who, if I walked past our cat as a small kid, would say, "Stop and pay him some attention. You're going to hurt his feelings." Now eighty-one and carless, she endures a long commute each week to comfort cats at the Humane Society. She's one of their best volunteers, largely because she's willing to show up on Boxing Day or Thanksgiving.

"The cats don't know it's a holiday," she'll explain if someone asks why she's giving up a special day. "To them, it's a weekday like any other."

Someone else might find this funny: cats thinking about the calendar like businessmen. But I don't see it that way. My favourite books when I was little – books I drew a huge amount of comfort from after my parents divorced – were classics like *Stuart Little* and *Charlotte's Web*, in which animals talked to each other and led lives far more interesting than mine. I still have my copy of *Puss in Boots*, and the cover, with its feisty tabby decked out in a cape, a swashbuckler's hat, and bejewelled jaunty boots, still seems totally logical to me. If a cat's going on an adventure, *of course* he needs a decent hat and boots.

I've been teased about this attitude for much of my life. In law school, I had a friend who'd transferred out of a post-doc in neuroscience. Part of his earlier research had involved monitoring cat brains – that is, slicing off a chunk of the cat's head, attaching electrodes to its brain, and then leaving the brain exposed. When I asked if this disturbed him, he looked at me like I had several screws loose.

"Of course not. Cats don't have personalities. They're just . . ." Raymond was possibly smarter than me, and very articulate, but he wasn't able to finish his sentence. "There's nothing *there*," he concluded, as if his point were self-evident.

"*My* cat has a personality," I replied. This was 1996, and I was talking about Hodge Podge, a black-and-white cat I'd adopted a year earlier and who I loved so much the thought of life without him felt like going blind.

"You're making that up," Ray replied.

This was another criticism I'd been on the receiving end of for a long time – my tendency to daydream and fantasize. Raymond couldn't be accused of this. He had a Ph.D. in neuroscience. He was a realist. He didn't jolt with a start in the middle of a lecture only to realize he had no recollection of where he'd been for the past twenty minutes.

The two criticisms often fused: animals mattered to me *because* I had such a tenuous grip on reality. If I'd just wake up, I'd see them as any other ordinary object, like a tablecloth or a chair.

I sometimes worried about this myself: was my tendency to view animals as human the sign of a lazy mind? But then I'd think of Dakota, or Hodge, or Kisu Cat, the majestic Siamese I'd had the luck of growing up with, and decide that if my thinking was a sign of weakness, it was a weakness that made my life richer.

It's an important point for any belongingness project. I think we're all told, in one way or another, that something that matters to us shouldn't really matter. Dirt bikes? Animals? A fascination with windup clocks? Belonging is always rooted through what we value. Which means that if you let other people tell you what you should or should not care about, you'll wind up cut off, or struggling with a sense of connection that never feels quite real. And it can be hard not to give in to other people's judgments. I sometimes still think of Raymond and worry that he had some special insight I lack. Then I tell myself to stop. If you think that something matters, then it does matter, and the worst thing you can do in any search for connection is push that thing aside.

This doesn't mean that it's *easy* to create a sense of connection through what you value. The Jack Russell group, for instance, presented immediate problems. The website was matter of fact: Russells on TV are professionally trained, most are high-strung, and they possess a strong prey drive.

I glanced at Hodge, who was sitting beside my computer as I read. He was now sixteen years old, and his kidneys were failing, meaning he was mostly skin and bones. Subjecting him to a Jack Russell, even one that didn't bite, seemed cruel. I was his, and he was mine, and he needed me during what were going to be the last years of his life.

I leaned forward to give him a kiss – he always smelled of warm wool – and clicked over to the Humane Society page. One of the things I'd loved to do on the coast was walk strays, but those had been mostly hunting dogs like beagles and coonhounds. Toronto dogs were different. The province had banned pit bulls in 2005, but people had tried to breed their way around the ban. This meant the pound was full of mixed breeds like Staffordshire Terrier–Labrador crosses: dogs that weren't entirely menacing but were halfway there.

I couldn't walk a dog like this – big dogs scare me – so I called the Humane Society with a question.

"I'd love to walk dogs," I said. "But I'm wondering if I could just walk the small ones?"

"No," the receptionist said absently.

"Why not?"

"Because there aren't enough small dogs to walk. There's lots of people who ask about that, but we get the big breeds. You have to be able to handle them."

I fell silent, and the receptionist seemed to feel she'd let me down.

"There's a cat care session coming up," she said, in a conciliatory tone. She didn't add, *You should probably be able to handle a kitten*, but the suggestion was there.

Fine. I asked when it was, and she told me to attend on a Saturday in early October.

The smell was exactly as I remembered it from when I had adopted Hodge there sixteen years earlier – airlessness combined with ammonia and a hint of pee. The place was dark and unadorned, with bricked-in windows that made the front desk feel like the entrance to a nuclear site. Someone had tried to liven the place up with LCD screens showing pictures of available pets, but the screens were near the ceiling, and the animals looked vulnerable so high up in the air.

When I asked about the orientation session, the receptionist, without even looking at me, said, "Second floor. Can't miss it."

As soon as I got upstairs, I understood what she meant. I couldn't see the meeting room, because the crowd inside was overflowing out of its two side doors and into the hall. I could hear a woman in the room saying things like "enrichment" and "guidelines," but my view was blocked by all the people standing in front of the doors and in the hallway. There were windows upstairs, but they weren't open, and I was starting to feel too warm in my hiking boots and corduroy jacket.

The crowd made me realize that animals matter to a lot of people. I'm sure that everyone there wanted more animal contact in their lives. But part of me wondered if even a small fraction of the people present were there because they'd read some self-help writings on connection. There's a lot in this literature about nurturing, showing compassion, or just being nice. Behaving in these ways is supposed to release the hormone oxytocin, which triggers feelings of calm connectedness and trust. One way to boost oxytocin levels is to have sex, but most articles settle on a more family-friendly example: mothers who have just given birth are flooded with the stuff. With both sex and childbirth often hard to come by, however, writers need to point to more accessible ways of getting an oxytocin hit, and caring for animals is almost always at the top of the list.

I'm not sure the self-help writers are wrong. Spending time with animals *does* feel good. But other experts – such as those who work in the field of animal-assisted therapy – stress that the feel-good effect isn't hormonal so much as psychological. Animals present no real threat of rejection. A dog might snap or behave unpredictably, but it's hard to imagine a Dalmatian looking at you as if to say, *I can't believe you're wearing that.* Working with animals leads to connection not because we've suddenly adopted the physiological profile of a new mom, but because we've let our guards down: with no sense of pending judgment, we let ourselves reach out and show emotions in ways we might not feel safe or secure enough to do with other people.

I understood all of this; I just didn't want to hang around with the crowd outside the meeting room. With nothing to hear, it was boring. So I left the hall and headed to the cat adoption area itself.

Here, the windows were open, and it was nice to walk in to fresh air and sunlight. There was a certain harshness to the scene – cats were stacked in rows, and each cage had thin, prison-like bars down the front. But the cages were big and clean, and they were filled with food, toys, and climbing posts. There were a few "cat cuddlers" – all women – settled on mats along the edge of the room, gently stroking or playing with cats on the floor. I liked these women immediately: I admired their desire to make even a small difference. Every cat had a bio attached to its cage, a sort of short story about how it had wound up there. One woman was sitting beside the open cage of a cat whose bio started with the all-caps word PALLIATIVE. She'd lifted the thin old cat to the ground and was patting and reassuring him as he made his way toward the window. I had to look away. The cat reminded me too much of Hodge, and the woman's affection for a creature with no future made something within me swerve. I wasn't sure I'd be able to open myself up in that way.

I later went on to confront my tendency to turn away from what hurt, but at that point I was just looking at the scene and thinking, (a) *I can't do this*, and (b) *Something feels off*. When I had told my mother I was going to the training session, she had suggested, as a "cat cuddler" herself, that this might not be the best idea.

"Honey," she said. "You'd be bored out of your *mind*." It was always hard to pin down my mother's accent, especially since it tended to change in keeping with how tired she was. Raised in the Midwest, with much of her adulthood spent in Kentucky, she had drawn-out vowels and a hint of twang. But mainly, she just sounded *different*. She was eighteen before TVs appeared, and she never got the hang of speaking in the flatter, more standardized tones of broadcasters. Like my dad, she'd grown up poor, only hers was a less scenic poverty, since it took place in Minneapolis and meant she'd had to get a job at eleven. But she talked about this job with affection. She'd worked in a drugstore, and one of her tasks had been to stand in the doorway and call out the names of streetcars so that customers wouldn't miss their trams. At eighty-one, she still sounded like someone from that era, with her how-can-I-help-you voice hinting at trolley cars, dimestore novels, thick nylons, and uniformed GIs.

"Can you really see yourself spending three hours patting cats?" she asked. She wasn't trying to criticize. She just didn't think it was realistic.

"Well, you do it."

"Yes. And on some days the cats are so depressed that nothing happens. I can't see you sitting through that."

"I can."

"Well, now . . . ," she said, trailing off. I was famous in my family for once waking Terri to calm me after what I called a "terrible nightmare." I was about seven at the time.

"Was it a monster?" Terri asked, coming to sit on my bed. She was always quick to offer comfort. "Was someone coming after you?"

"No," I cried. "It was a *blanket*."

She pried the details out of me. In the dream, I was working at a factory and holding my hand to an unspooling sheet of cloth. My job was to make sure the cloth was perfectly smooth.

"And then what?" Terri asked.

"Nothing," I said, terrified. "It was my *job*."

I couldn't explain myself very well, because the word *monotony* hadn't yet entered my vocabulary. But that was what scared me: the possibility of being caught in a situation that never changed. My mother understood this, and although she was tactful enough to not bring up what had become known as Emily's Weird Dream, she made it clear that she thought cat cuddling was the wrong fit.

"You need more stimulation," she concluded.

The conversation was coming back to me as I stood in the cat adoption room. Was she right? I wasn't sure. Filled with something close to a childlike urge to rebel, I decided to push the issue. This was a mistake. I've come to learn that sometimes the people closest to us can spot problems we can't see, and I eventually started to pay more attention to what those around me had to say about belonging, and what they saw as the best way of going after it.

At that point, though, I was still relying on my instincts alone, so I went back to the orientation session. It was over. In fact, it seemed to have been over for some time. People were still milling around the hallway, but many others had left. I was able to enter the room itself for the first time. It was hot and smelled like damp shoes. All the surfaces were wipe-down, and I had a vision of a volunteer coming in to sterilize it in much the same way that the cages were cleaned. The coordinator – a flush-faced twentysomething looking totally overwhelmed – was collecting sheets of paper from people.

"What is that?" I asked, leaning over someone seated at one of the hose-down tables.

"The form."

"Where do you get it?"

His English wasn't very strong, but he was helpful enough in pointing toward the coordinator.

I had to sidle my way into a conversation she was having. In fact, I was getting dirty looks for what people saw as butt-ing in line. I wondered why people were queuing – there was a stack of filled-out forms on the table, and all anyone had to do was drop theirs off. Then I realized that there were far more applicants than there were positions. People wanted face time to make their applications stand out.

"Sorry," I said, interrupting the conversation and earn-ing more dirty looks. "Could I just get a sheet?"

The young woman handed me one while barely glancing at me. This wasn't rude. She just seemed dazed, like she'd been expecting twenty volunteers and still hadn't adjusted to the fact that over eighty had shown up.

I found a spot at a table and picked up a dull pencil that someone had left behind. Some of the questions, I'd expected – name, age, "cat experience." This was all fill-in-the-blanks type stuff. But then, to my surprise, came something closer to an essay question: "What special qualifications do you have that would make you a good candidate for volunteer work at the Humane Society?"

The question struck me as strange. I'd already filled in "cat experience," writing that I'd lived with cats for forty years. Feeling playful, I had added, "cat whisperer." What "special qualifications" did I need beyond this? Cat CPR? Rescuing kittens from burning buildings?

It was clear that the Humane Society was screening. The fact that the agency wasn't charging for a sense of connection meant it was overrun. Which meant, in turn, that it had to find a way of weeding people out, and it was doing so by posing a question so opaque that a lot of people were going to throttle themselves answering it.

I actually could answer it. I'd been chair of the Animals and the Law club at my law school and had spent years as a card-carrying member of the Animal Legal Defense Fund. If that didn't lift my application to the top of the pile, I thought, nothing would.

But I wasn't sure that was fair. There were about ten people still seated at the tables, filling out forms, and another five waiting to chat up the coordinator. Many of these people seemed stressed – clutching their forms tightly, or smiling too broadly, or trying to explain, often in broken English, why they wanted to help. Some of these stories sounded borderline desperate – "Here, I am all alone" – and this reminded me that some people really needed this work.

I wasn't in that kind of situation. I didn't just have social ties, I had Hodgie, and I knew that my low-key landlord wouldn't object if I ever decided to adopt a second cat to increase my daily contact with animals. I sat back in my plastic chair and started tapping my pencil over and over against the form, creating a pointillist look that would probably disqualify me on grounds of being crazy. I knew I wanted a form of belonging that was linked to animals. But I wasn't sure it had to take the form of cat cuddling. I was vaguely aware of other groups – organizations that grabbed feral cats off the street, or fed homeless colonies, or fostered straight-from-the-track greyhounds. I also had a sense, which turned out to be right, that if I tried to pursue my goal in a less mainstream way, I'd have an easier time belonging, simply because I wouldn't be competing for scarce positions.

I thought of the second leg of Hagerty's Rule and realized that in this case, the fit was wrong. This didn't mean that my goal was wrong. It just meant I had to be more creative. I think this is where a lot of people get stuck searching for connection. They head to a group they think they should belong to – a soup kitchen, a tutoring outfit – and realize

they don't particularly want to be there. Then they stop.
That's where the mistake comes in. The trick is to keep your
main goal in mind – mine was loosely *animals* – and try to
approach it in a different way. Go online and google groups
related to your interests. Put your goal at the centre of a
sheet of paper and brainstorm. Ask around. This requires
more work than joining the first thing that comes to mind,
but it also leads to a greater sense of connection.

In the end, I folded the piece of paper and shoved it
into my pocket. No one noticed me leaving. I felt better
knowing that I hadn't taken a spot away from someone
who really needed it, and I knew that my overall goal was
still worthwhile. But as I got home, eager to find a way to
connect via animals, I felt uncomfortable. There was an
edginess and a sense of not quite fitting in that hit the
second I walked in the door. I often felt more belonging –
or at least less of a sense of *not* belonging – in places more
neutral than my apartment; even stalled subways sometimes felt more comfortable than my own living room.
I looked around and couldn't understand it. I had a very
nice living room. Hodge came to greet me and we sat
together on the floor.

I'm going to sound totally anthropomorphic here –
as loosey-goosey as my old law school classmate once
suggested – but it seemed as if Hodge wasn't totally comfortable in the space, either. When we had first moved in,
he'd often woken me up at night, howling as he walked
down the hall. We'd both lost our home, of course; we'd
both landed in the apartment in the rush of change that

had followed my separation. But it went deeper than that.
I couldn't settle, and I knew that until I did, Hodge wouldn't
settle, either. We were both cut off, disconnected, and the
thing we were missing was *home*.

CHAPTER TWO

Home

Creating a Base for Belonging and Getting Past the Past

THE MISMATCH BETWEEN the way I felt at home and the way I felt I *should* feel at home was dizzying. If there had been something wrong with the apartment, I could have said, *I can't connect here because of the awful linoleum, the horrendous paint job, the total lack of light*. As it was, I was living in a spacious, airy place that caught the sun all day long. My flat was on the top floor of an eighty-year-old house and featured the original walnut flooring, a beautiful built-in wardrobe, and dark woodwork around all the windows and doors. There was a huge deck off the kitchen that overlooked a park, and the apartment was arranged in the drawn-out style I like best, with a long hallway connecting the rooms and serving as a corridor for breezes that blew in from the back.

It was, all things considered, a find. The landlord, an older man with an undefined but clearly well-paying job in the arts, liked the idea of a writer in the house. There was some confusion about the rent – he'd posted two different prices on Craigslist – and when I pointed this out, he immediately went with the lower number. This meant the apartment wasn't just spacious but also cheap, an almost impossible combination in downtown Toronto, where tenant bidding wars break out over places half the size of mine.

The fact that the apartment was so undeniably great was discouraging, because it made me think there might be something wrong with me. I just couldn't feel any sense of home there. And this in turn made me wonder if there might be something more fundamentally off about me – that my inability to connect to home might be one aspect of a larger inability to connect at all.

Because home is the starting point for a sense of belonging. We tend to think of belonging as "out there," woven into the world around us. And it is out there, but the way we feel at home can affect the energy and attitudes we bring to that larger world. Researchers at the University of Maine created a clever experiment to test this point. The psychologists Sandra Sigmon and Stacy Whitcomb asked students to walk into a room that had only some bare essentials in it: a sofa, an armchair, a coffee table. They then gave the students access to posters, cushions, plants, books, and vases, and told each student to take as much time as necessary decorating the space. After leaving the room, each student was given tests assessing anxiety, well-being, and social confidence. When the researchers compared the finished rooms with the test scores, they found that students who spent more time decorating, and who set out the most objects with care, rated higher in terms of positive mood, reduced stress, and increased social energy.

Sigmon and Whitcomb suggested that something called "psychological home" was serving as the link between setting out a vase of flowers and having more social ties. By this, they meant that the way we relate to our home environment serves as a template for how we relate to the larger environment: the more at home and in charge you feel in your house or apartment, the more at home and in charge you'll feel outside of it. A separate study conducted at the University of Chicago came to the same conclusion. Polling over three hundred families, the sociologists Mihaly Csikszentmihalyi and Eugene Rochberg-Halton found that people who described their home environments as "warm" or "welcoming" were more likely to be out in the community, joining clubs or teams and attending neighbourhood events. People who described their homes as "cold" were much less likely to be part of school, sports, or neighbourhood groups, meaning – ironically – that it's the people who feel least at home who have the hardest time leaving it.

I had found this to be true in the psychological home experiment I'd inadvertently run on the coast. I lived in St. John's, Newfoundland, for five years before returning to Toronto. For two of those years, my ex and I lived in a house that was cold, damp, and dark. For most of those two years, I was basically a hermit. I taught courses at the university and went for walks, but usually I just cooped myself up in the one room that felt cozy and stayed put. Then, after an aggressive lobbying campaign on my part, Danielle and I moved to a bright, beautiful 125-year-old house set right beside a river. Light flooded the rooms; we had floor-to-ceiling windows that overlooked reeds and wild grasses; and our deck jutted out over the river itself. On nice mornings, I'd make coffee, grab Hodge, and head outside. The two of us would sit on the deck and stare out at the water, and I'd think that I had never been so happy in all my life.

As this feeling grew – as I came to love the old house with its ornate mouldings, basement kitchen, and pink shag runner on the stairs – I became socially bolder. I was friendlier with the neighbours; I joined a meditation class; I signed up for belly dancing and a writing group; I walked strays. It was as if I were carrying that good sense of home with me wherever I went, as if the sense of belonging I found indoors was something I could project onto the world around me.

When I thought about it, I realized that *home* was a big part of the answer to the question Genevieve had posed: when had I felt a sense of belonging in the past? Here, my answer was much clearer than *dog*, because I could cite a specific address. The problem was, I wasn't sure how to recreate that feeling in Toronto. The sense of home that I'd felt in St. John's had seemed like a property of the house itself, something that would just impose itself on anyone lucky enough to live there.

Sigmon and Whitcomb, in their study on the relationship between home and social confidence, stressed that "home is a verb": it's something you have to *do*. I was willing to do things; I just wasn't sure what to do. The mechanics of home have never come easily to me. I'm not visually gifted, hammering prints to walls makes me nervous, and I'm a minimalist. Carefully decorated rooms – the sort the

Maine study linked to psychological and social well-being –
make me slightly uneasy.

It was clear that I had to get past this. With experts such as
Columbia University's Mindy Fullilove describing home as
the base of belonging, I knew that my overall challenge would
be much harder if I lacked a sense of home. So I reached out
for some advice. My closest friend, Laura, is a whiz at "doing
home." We met on our first day of law school in 1996, and
she spent the next three years acing courses while puttering
around her apartment. She made orange paper window
panels to catch the light; stripped and repainted a Goodwill
dresser (also orange); tore the linoleum off her bathroom
floor and buffed the ceramic tiles underneath; and tended to
so many plants that her place felt like a greenhouse.

If anyone could help me spot the sense of home in my
apartment, it was Laura. She said she was happy to help, and
that she was glad I'd reached out: a personal touch to home
struck her as important. "The last thing you want is one of
those TV shows where someone comes in and remakes
your whole place, and you go, 'Oh, my God.' It's like somebody helping you choose a wardrobe. They should maybe
push you a bit, but they shouldn't buy you a whole pink
wardrobe if you only wear earth tones."

Oddly enough, Laura's clothes were the first thing I
noticed when she appeared at my door one fall evening to
help me out with my home project. As she took off her
coat, I saw that she was wearing a tight top with a complicated neckline, as well as blush and mascara. I had to take a
moment to readjust.

For most of our friendship, we've matched: we're the same height, we wear our long hair in ponytails, and we even buy the same shoes (black Clarks, size nine). I like it that we match. In fact, over the course of this challenge, I came to realize just how important matching is to me. I love looking at my sister Chris and noticing how alike our cheekbones and jawlines are; I like hearing my mother's voice reflected in my own; and I like it when Juliette and I use the same phrases – "the crib," "dude," "awesome" – dating back to college or even earlier. Matching is comforting. In a world where belongingness rates are low, mirroring is a sign that you do belong, that others are just like you. One of the hardest things I had to do in this challenge was get past the idea that belonging *meant* matching; I had to learn that I could feel part of groups or neighbourhoods where people didn't look and act just like me.

However, that lesson was still some ways off, and Laura was one of my closest ties. The fact that we matched even a bit less than before bothered me, even though I understood the reason for the change. Having given up a career in human rights law to start her own business, Laura faced a fashion challenge. She'd joined several associations for female entrepreneurs and was suddenly around people *she* didn't match with. "I've gone from hanging out with women who never wear makeup to hanging out with women who always wear it," she'd explained a few months earlier. "And I have to make more of an impression on the businesswomen, so I'm trying to get used to it."

I was trying to get used to it too. Laura was the daughter of a travelling minister, and I thought scrubbed good looks suited her perfectly. But I also noticed how pretty she looked in blush and mascara, and over the course of the next few months, without giving the matter any conscious thought, I solved the problem of us not matching by buying blush and mascara myself.

At that point, though, makeup wasn't on my list of concerns. I needed Laura's advice on home and so stuck to the business at hand.

"Do you want me to think about what I'd do if this was my place?" she asked. We were standing in the kitchen, about to start a tour of my apartment, and I was holding a tape recorder up so that I didn't miss a thing.

"Exactly. Don't hold back. Describe anything you'd do."

Telling her not to hold back might have been a mistake. Laura had so many suggestions, it was like turning on a tap. She'd buy a new loveseat, add plants to the tops of bookcases, put a plush chair in the bedroom, hang the photos my dad had left me, do creative things with cushions, and add colour to my kitchen floor.

"A big mat would be nice in here," she said. We were back in the kitchen, and she was looking at my white table and floor. "But then you'd have the issue of, should the table be on the mat or off the mat?"

She was puzzling over this, clearly visualizing the mat in one spot and then the next, when I broke in.

"So you wouldn't have a problem with home here?" I asked.

She stared at me. She was bright-eyed and flushed, clearly energized by the mere thought of creating a home.

"This is a *great* place. It has so much potential. Don't tell my husband" – Laura had gotten married two years earlier and had moved to a large house – "but I think it would be *fun* to live here, to have a snug place again and all these cozy rooms."

I was trying to figure out why Laura and I – who matched in so many ways – were so different when it came to home.

"You're artistic," I said clumsily. "You've got an eye for colour. How much of that can someone cultivate without it coming automatically?"

She laughed. "I don't know. But I think you can cultivate it if you want to. And if you run into problems, you ask me, or you ask someone else. I don't think it's any more complicated than you not committing yourself to the space."

"I have been feeling kind of ambivalent about that," I replied.

"Listen," she said, taking the tape recorder from me. "I think you're being too hard on yourself. I can imagine you doing this. You're not incapable of making a comfortable home for yourself. You're more on the sparse side than I am, but you can do it."

I wasn't sure she was right. I didn't know if I could live up to my home-making potential. And Laura was always so helpful, so ready to assist. It took everything I had not to ask, *Listen, please, could you just move in for a week and do this* for *me?*

One reason I didn't say this was that asking a friend, even a close friend who loves home-making, to redecorate your entire apartment is asking a bit too much. But I was also struck by Laura's reference to commitment. She had said that the problem wasn't a lack of skill; it was that I was hedging.

This interested me, since it aligned with another major idea about belonging. If the Maine home decor experiment was about *doing*, other work has been about *thinking*. In 1990, psychologist Brian Lakey, then at Wayne State University, became interested in the question of how much belonging we might be toting around with us. To probe this question, he gave students a list and asked them to check off the various forms of support they'd received from others in the past month; he then asked them to describe how much support they felt they'd received. The descriptions didn't jibe. Many students who were surrounded by helpful people didn't feel this way at all: they felt like they were on their own. In a follow-up experiment, students were asked to think about a situation that called for social support (your boyfriend has just left you) and then given an example of the support someone might offer (you're invited over for dinner). Even though all the students were given the same scenarios and the same examples of support, only some students saw that support as helpful; others were untouched.

Lakey went on to suggest that our sense of the world as a supportive place, one in which other people are there for us, is only partly tied to what's happening in the world. A good chunk of our sense of connection or support might be flowing from how we view our interactions. If we don't notice what we're projecting onto those interactions – and that might be distrust, uneasiness, or dismissal – we can start to feel like something's missing, even when, objectively, it's not.

From a practical standpoint, Lakey argued that a person might achieve a greater sense of inclusion by focusing on what's happening internally, rather than by trying to reshape the world around him or her. A massive follow-up study conducted at the University of Chicago found that Lakey was right. When the scientists Christopher Masi and John Cacioppo looked at what worked best in helping people feel less alone, the most effective strategy they hit on was changing *thoughts*. It's not that getting to know more people doesn't help. It's that you'll get more of a boost from that bigger social circle, and be able to latch onto it more firmly, if you see the new people you meet as helpful, interesting, and trustworthy.

In a sense, there's no clear dividing line between the idea of belonging as something we work for and the idea of it as something we perceive, and that's because our perceptions influence how much energy we have to do the work. But even though doing and perceiving were forming a feedback loop in my head, I felt the need to hack the circle open. Because I still wasn't sure what the main problem was. Was I just not trying hard enough at home? Or was I not trying hard enough because I didn't believe that home would ever be there?

Trying struck me as a slightly easier thing to assess than perception. So, shortly after Laura's visit, I made a resolution to "do" home. I wrote out all the things she'd suggested, and I also made a trip to the big box bookstore near my house to see what professionals had to say about home. As I flipped through glossy magazines, I made an executive decision to skip the pure fantasy stuff – the cedar-lined soaker tubs, calligraphy studios, and fields of grazing horses – and I also, a bit more reluctantly, turned the page on anything that struck me as out of character. The idea of holding a sage-burning ceremony in my bedroom was intriguing, but I'd also thought the LSAT was fun, and I decided that trying to remodel my living room and my personality at the same time was too much even for me.

My personality was more in sync with practical advice, and this was abundantly available. There was no shortage of publications telling me to focus on colour, feel, and layout. Words like *life* and *scent* also popped up a lot; flowers were a recurring theme. I winnowed the suggestions into a list of things that felt workable and then tried to put as many of these ideas as possible into practice.

When my birthday arrived, for instance, I asked for candles and perfumed soaps, in order to create a spa-like effect in my bathroom. My mother, sensing the direction I was headed in, gave me fluffy towels and a thick bath mat as well. When I put everything out, the room looked great, but it felt like a stage set. I didn't take many baths and I usually showered at the gym, so I couldn't quite remember why I'd asked for those particular gifts. I bought cream-coloured curtains for the living room, but they blocked too much light, so I took them down. My aromatherapy diffuser was too strong, so I set it on the deck to air and raccoons kicked it over, leaving me with a half-empty jar and planks smelling nicely of rosewater. I bought tulips, but I mistakenly put them in a carafe instead of a vase. It turns out there is a difference. The carafe's neck was so narrow, the flowers choked; four days into my "beautification" experiment, I was staring at mould around the bottle's neck and flowers that had clearly breathed their last. I bought frames for the photographs my dad had left me, but I was flummoxed to realize that they needed picture wire, which I didn't have. So I wound up stacking them on my trunk, telling myself I'd get to them later and knowing I never would.

Sitting in Juliette and Andrew's lushly furnished living room one evening, I tried to explain the problem. "I've bought all this stuff, but it just feels like stuff. I like the photos, but I've had them for years. Nothing new seems to matter very much."

Talking about home with Juliette and Andrew was like talking about psychotherapy with Freud. They just *were* the authority. Their own home – a big Victorian three-storey – could have been cold: it was poorly insulated and the rooms were linked like rail cars. But as soon as you walked in, you were met with muted colours and soft fabrics and an overall sense of being in the space of two people who cared deeply about where they lived, and who were welcoming to others as well.

"It's not just about buying things," Andrew said. His yoga-toned body was long and lean, and he was sitting elegantly in a wing-backed chair. Juliette matched him – long and lean herself, she was sitting with her legs crossed in the chair opposite his. I was flat out on the sofa, my hair sprawled everywhere and my hands pressed to the sides of my head like I was trying to solve a complicated geometric puzzle.

"Or, people think it is," Andrew continued. "That's why Williams-Sonoma catalogues work. People think, *If I just had a three-foot paella pan and a Viking stove, then my loved ones would gather round me and we'd have this awesome, soulful experience.* But of course it doesn't work like that."

"So I shouldn't buy anything? You guys have a lot of stuff." The house was richly decorated: Chinese screens on the walls, an antique table, and a sofa – the one I was lying on – so soft it made standing seem completely overrated.

"It's not about never buying things," Andrew said, correcting himself. "But if you're going to buy things, you should use them, and if you're going to use them, they should bring you pleasure. It doesn't sound like anything you bought does that for you."

"Bring pleasure?"

"You know why you like that sofa so much?" Juliette asked. My love of their sofa was well known. When I house-sat for them, I slept on it. "It's because I sat on half the couches in Toronto. And didn't stop until I found one that I absolutely loved."

Love. Pleasure. The words were more sensual than Laura's stock phrase, "If this were my apartment, I'd do this," but they were prompting the same sort of anxiety.

Juliette was trying to explain the strategy she'd used to learn how to love the homes she was in. An arty ex-boy-friend had bought her a stack of home magazines and a scrapbook. Juliette was to cut out anything she liked – any photo at all – and staple it into the scrapbook on the appro-priate page, be it "bathroom," "bedroom," or "kitchen."

"And I realized I did have a style. I was drawn to so much white, and lots of clean lines, with just hints of colour. And once I realized I had a style, it was easier for me to recognize what I liked. So I was more sure of myself."

I understood what Juliette was saying – if you're going to seek things that bring you pleasure, it helps, as a preliminary step, to know what it is you like – but I already knew my style. I thought of it loosely as Rich Person's Cottage, and it was modelled on the cottage of a real rich person I'd dated for years in my early twenties. Martin's mother could have taken Martha Stewart to school. The family cottage was made of huge beams reclaimed from an abandoned farmhouse, and it had been furnished with overstuffed gingham sofas, clever fish carvings, and an earnestly plain monk's table bought for an outrageous sum from an actual monastery. *That* was my style.

But there was a problem, I realized. It wasn't just cost (though, done right, Rich Person's Cottage was out of my price range). It was that I didn't want to buy things. This wasn't an offshoot of my "don't buy belonging" rule; the prospect of buying things just made me jumpy.

After my conversation with Juliette and Andrew, I did spot a small hallway table that I forced myself to purchase. I then stood watching as the delivery man hauled it up my stairs.

"It's a nice piece," he said, counting my money.

It was nice. Its dark wood matched my floors, and it had delicate fluted legs and a flat side that sat perfectly against the wall. From a decor perspective, it fit the space perfectly. But I was suddenly overwhelmed with the urge to ask the delivery man to take it back. I started scrambling for an excuse. What could be wrong with it? I pressed my hand down to see if it wobbled, but it was flush with the floor.

"You're going?" I asked as he turned around. He looked a bit surprised. Was I expecting him to stay?

"Yes," he said, still looking puzzled.

"Okay," I replied, a bit sadly. I did not want to be alone with my table.

I followed the driver down the steps and then watched from the doorway as he headed toward his van. Since the delivery was such a quick one, he hadn't bothered parking properly. The end of the van was jutting into the road, and as he headed down my walk, a second car came along and struck his. I heard tail lights shatter, and the delivery man swear, and I instantly swung the door shut and slid down out of sight. I was convinced that if the driver could see me he'd blame me for the accident, and that I'd better not do anything else about home or something *awful* would happen.

This strange reaction – feeling I'd caused the accident through the simple act of attending to home – made me seriously reconsider my whole approach. I began to look at my home project from a psychological point of view. Maybe there was something about my perceptions that made belonging to home – and possibly belonging in general – just too fraught and scary for me to reach out for.

Psychological research on home began in the 1970s, when UC Berkeley professor Clare Cooper Marcus noticed that some people connected to home very easily, while others didn't. She saw this difference as meaningful. People who couldn't connect to home, she believed, were projecting something onto their environment: a lack of connection in general, the experience of trauma, or a low sense of self-worth, for example. This is a radically different notion from the one set out in magazines and home decor manuals, which suggests a pretty environment affects *us*. Marcus's thinking on home aligned with Lakey's thinking on support and belonging, particularly the idea that a good chunk of these concepts is in our heads, and if we're not aware of the ideas we're bringing to home, we can trip ourselves up without even noticing.

To tease out what they were really thinking when they heard the word *home*, Marcus got people interacting with the idea in new ways: she asked people to draw it, talk to it, and ask it what it had to say.

After the "I caused an accident by buying a small table" incident, it was clear that I had to try these things myself. Marcus's main piece of advice is to draw your home and then place the drawing in a chair and sit across from it. You talk to the chair. You then fall silent and let the drawing talk to you. I felt unnerved but strangely obedient when faced with these instructions. It was weird, but I was going to do it.

I drew my home using coloured pencils. After I finished, I sat back and immediately noticed that although I live in a duplex attached to another house, I'd drawn a completely freestanding structure. Not only did I not have any neighbours, but the house itself was floating a few inches above the ground, completely unrooted. This seemed like such an uncanny representation of my emotional life – just not grounded and connected enough – that I was momentarily alarmed. It was like going from not believing in fortune-telling to having a palm reader describe every detail of your life. Did I really *want* to know what my house had to say?

I decided I needed to. I placed the picture on a chair. It fell over. I taped it to a Jonathan Franzen novel and put it back in place.

"Hello," I said.

Silence.

"I don't know what to say," I continued. This was true. This was my first experience in talking to a chair.

More silence.

"This is awkward," I admitted. "We don't have much of a relationship."

"That's because you don't want one." This was the chair talking. Its voice took me by surprise. I mean, it was clearly my voice, but I really just felt like a channel for what it had to say.

"I do want a relationship," I replied, speaking as myself again. "I just don't know how to create one."

"You're not trying."

I took some offence to this. "I *am* trying. I just can't fix what's wrong."

"What's wrong?"

Without realizing it, I repeated what Laura had said, because it felt true.

"I can't commit to you."

"Why not?"

Now it was my turn for silence. I knew what I had to say – the words were crammed up in my throat – but I didn't want to say them, because I found them upsetting.

"Because if I do, I'm going to lose you."

Silence. The mention of loss seemed to have shut down our conversation. There was nothing for the drawing to say back to me. Had I said the wrong thing, or possibly too much? I felt suddenly gauche, like I'd put the drawing in an awkward spot.

I tried once more. "Hello?"

More silence. Our talk was clearly over. I tore the drawing off of *Freedom* and flipped through the book. I wanted distraction, but I was already distracted by something else. I felt like I'd come close to something crucial, but whatever it was was so big that I couldn't properly see it. I finally gave up and put the book away, telling myself my whole project was hopeless. Then I looked around the living room, saw the orange throw Laura had set on the back of an armchair, and thought, *Well, at least I have an accent colour.*

I might have remained like this indefinitely if I hadn't accidentally come across a book in the research library. I'd decided to take a break from wrestling with my home and think instead about belonging to local place, and in the section on cities and sprawl there was a slim volume called *Returning Home*. It was about adults going back to their childhood homes – sometimes crossing oceans or driving for days to get there. I was captivated and read half the book on my knees in the stacks.

As soon as I got back to my problematic apartment, I sent an email to the author, Santa Clara University professor Jerry Burger, and asked if I could talk to him. My motives weren't clear to me, even as I hit "send." I talk to a lot of experts, but usually I have a specific question in mind. With Burger, I just wanted to hear his voice. Even though I couldn't name the problem facing me, I felt that talking to him might give me some clue.

"Hi," he said affably, when I called the next day. He sounded warm and generous. I knew he'd probably answer whatever I asked. A lot of the ideas he'd presented in the book were in line with place attachment. The basic idea here is that connecting to place and connecting to people are not two different things: lessons about people are always learned in a place, and lessons about place can be taught by people. This is why the Maine experiment – which was about a room – could slide over into predictions about social ties. Feeling safe and comfortable with place can be a model for how we relate to people; feeling safe and comfortable with people can be a model for how we relate to place.

What fascinated me about Burger's research was his discussion of people who had returned to their childhood homes to find them gone. As soon as I read his passage about the experience of arriving to nothing, I thought of the scene in *Grosse Pointe Blank* where John Cusack drives to his childhood address only to find a convenience store.

"How do they feel?" I asked, referring to the people who'd lost their homes.

"Well, for a lot of people, it's pretty hard. Especially if they were expecting the home to be there – if they didn't know it had been demolished. A lot of people describe real grief."

"That happened to me, you know." I wasn't sure why I was telling him this. It wasn't anything I usually mentioned to anyone, let alone a stranger on the other end of a long-distance line.

"That's difficult," he said.

"Not just my home," I clarified. For some reason, I wanted him to have the whole story. "My whole neigh-bourhood. They tore down everything."

"Everything?"

"All of it. My house, all my neighbours' houses, the trees, my school, the church, the roads." There was some-thing odd about the way I was speaking. My heart was rac-ing, but my tone was flat. The table was starting to look far away, like I was viewing it through a pinhole. I wondered if this was what people meant by *dissociation*. It certainly felt like my brain and my voice were no longer associating.

Burger fell silent. I knew why I'd called him. He was the High Priest of Lost Houses. He'd know what to say. He could tell me, in the way that no magazine could, what I should *do*.

"Should I go back?" I asked, a bit tentatively.

He was cautious himself in responding. "Well, if there's so little left, it might be challenging. But if you're willing to settle for what you find, it could still be worthwhile."

"So go?" I felt like I needed a distinct instruction.

"You take what you can get," he advised.

I took this as a yes. That winter afternoon, I packed my "belongingness bag": notebook, fleecy vest, hat, water bottle, two energy bars. This was overkill – I was only travelling four subway stops north – but I felt in need of fortification. I boarded my northbound train like Shackleton leaving the *Endurance*. I wasn't sure what I was going to find, but I was going to face it.

What I found was confusion. The subway exit was the same, but as soon as I reached street level, everything was different. I'd grown up in a low-density, postwar suburb. The tallest things around had been the church steeple and a mall with seven stories of apartments on top. That was all gone. The developers who had arrived in the early 1980s had wanted more density, and they'd gotten it. There were high-rise condos and office towers in every direction, and the fact that so many were clad in mirrored glass made them seem like they were circling in on each other, as if one was about to spring on the next.

Feeling like a cat surrounded by enormous objects, I carefully made my way to my old street. All the landmarks were gone and the roads had been widened and reconfigured. Without the street sign, I'm not sure I would have recognized my road. The factory that used to sit north of the house had given way to three condo towers. The factory's parking lot was now a dog park. There was too much noise – the nearby highway seemed vastly louder than it had in my childhood – and there were way too many people around. My old 'hood had been home to about two hundred families. There were now easily three thousand people in the area, and these people seemed to be everywhere – jogging in all-weather gear, talking into cellphones, or steering into underground garages that hadn't previously existed.

I couldn't find my house. I knew it had been torn down, but I was having a hard time picturing where it used to be. A row of townhomes now abutted the street, and I walked down a faux laneway – all wrought-iron gates and leafless hedges – and tried to count off the steps from the crossroad. I wound up on a sidewalk, with traffic rushing past, and stopped across from where my house should have been. If I had the pacing right, there was nothing at all in its place. It was a sort of entryway, all shovelled out and grey, marked with a big stone slab that said WELCOME. I took one step forward, toward the sign, and then climbed back to the safety of the sidewalk. Whatever it was they had back there – more towers, more parking, perhaps a whole other town operating in a different dimension – I wasn't up for visiting.

This left me with nothing to do. I reached in my bag for an energy bar and ripped the wrapper off. I'm not an emotional eater, but I felt the strong need for a sugar fix right then. I was feeling low-energy, unfocused. Part of me could still see my old house – the pines my mother had planted, the red front door, the warm yellow bricks. It was the opposite of ordinary vision: when I closed my eyes, I could see the house; when I opened my eyes, it was gone. And this trick vision, with something vanishing the moment I looked, reminded me of how I used to feel as a child.

My parents divorced when I was four. No one told me
what was happening. After I'd grown up, my father said he
didn't think a four-year-old would understand the word
divorce, so he never explained why he was leaving. He also
never said goodbye. I just woke up one day to find my
father gone. But I'm not sure that my four-year-old mind
understood that he was gone. My childhood home was big,
and for a long time I had the sense that if I just turned the
right corner, or peeked into the right room, my dad would
be there with his arms open, telling me he'd been there all
along. The fact that this never happened didn't mean I
wasn't *expecting* it to happen, and the expectation left the
house feeling extra empty, as if someone were constantly
on their way out.

And my father's departure had a domino effect, since as a
result, others had to leave the house too. As a single mother,
my mom had to get a job, and when I was about six, she
found one that required long hours downtown. Chris, who
was nine years older than me, left for college when I was
eight. Terri didn't vanish, but she was a teenager, and I didn't
expect her to stay home with me when she could be out
with friends or boys. This meant that by the time I was nine,
I often walked in the back door to be confronted with aloneness and that sense of an absent presence.

Then this house that made people disappear pulled the
ultimate magic trick and disappeared itself. If my dad's vanishing happened overnight, the house's vanishing took
much longer. From the age of ten on, I watched my mother
and all our neighbours struggle to hang on to their homes.

There were drop boxes organized for letters; petitions were passed around. There were threats of lawsuits, actual lawsuits, signs of hope, and then the crash: the factory behind us decided to sell. If we didn't want to be the sole homeowners in a sea of towers, we'd better sell as well. The high-pitched hum of anxiety that had surrounded the house for years fell silent. It was over. My mom signed the sale agreement in 1988. I left for college that year and never saw the house again.

It's amazing how much of your life can be staring you in the face before you even notice it. I always told myself that losing my home in my teens didn't matter. I made no connection between that loss and the fact that I went on to become a "place" lawyer – fighting for the preservation of wetlands and fields, desperately trying to stop more losses from piling up. I also failed to notice how hard it was to repeatedly lose places – how decisions allowing for clear-cuts or highways would leave me flat on my back on my office floor, awash with the same sadness that was setting in right then in front of the empty space where my home had been.

I wanted to sit on the sidewalk, but it was too cold. So I just stood there. I'd pulled out my notebook to write everything down, but my hand was cramped and I had no energy. That's how my adventure ended: with me alone on the side of the road, my pen out but not moving, staring at a place I'd lost in stages, a place that was now fully gone.

I think there's a lot of truth to the notion of belonging as work. But I also think that perceptions matter, and that some of us have been taught to see belonging as something risky, as something that might get taken away. Once that lesson has been learned, it can be hard to create a more connected life for yourself, especially if you're not aware of the lesson still doing its work.

I originally saw this as a problem unique to me. *How many people lose their homes?* I thought. But as soon as I started talking about it – and once the story was at the forefront of my mind, I wanted to talk about it all the time – I often started by saying, "This might be a hard thing to imagine," only to be met with, "No, I get it. The same thing happened to me." For my friend Gary, it was the loss of hectares of Georgia farmland that had been in his family for generations (now a subdivision). For my aunt, it was the loss of her Louisville neighbourhood (now an airport). For Laura, it was the loss of a town she'd grown up in (still technically there, but with the Ford plant shuttered, dying a slow and painful death).

Loss of place is critical. If you can't trust the ground under your feet to remain the same, what can you trust? But the twinning of loss and connection can occur in any area: the job that disappears, the spouse who leaves, the friend who departs for war and doesn't come back. And these stories about losing connection can become the stories we tell about connection itself – that it's not worth reaching out for because it will just disappear, or can't be counted on, or will just fall apart the instant you find it.

This was the story I was telling myself. Heck, I wasn't even telling myself. I was sitting in a chair and telling a *drawing* I couldn't commit to it. My reasoning went like this: if I committed to my apartment, it would vanish. This was not an irrational expectation. Buildings get demolished; cities gentrify; houses are sold. In my case, I'd grown up watching people disappear from place, and then – in something bordering on a hallucination – watching place itself disappear.

The only thing that puzzled me was why this story hadn't played itself out in Newfoundland. I had felt instantly at home in that riverside house. I'd had no problem with commitment. In fact, I had committed so quickly, and so hard, that when I had been forced to leave it had felt like cutting off a limb.

I felt the sudden need to see that house. I typed the address into Google Street View, and there it was, its paint bright blue and its shutters a cheerful white. There was a new planter on the front step, which Danielle had filled with petunias and red coleus. Otherwise, the place looked unchanged.

Still there, I thought. Then I realized that *this* was the story the house I loved had been telling me. Built in 1891, it had survived the huge fire that gutted the town in 1892, and it had gone on to survive generations of wind, rain, and hurricanes. I'd been there for one of these storms – Hurricane Igor, which hit in 2010. The hurricane saw me in my neighbour's yard, both of us pressed up against her oil tank, trying to keep the wind from tearing it into the river. This was an impossible task: the rain was flying sideways, the wind was blowing at over one hundred miles an hour, and if we stayed out any longer, one of us was going to end up in the drink. As I came in from the storm, the screaming wind gave way to near-total silence. *It might be madness outside*, the house seemed to say, *but all is safe and sound within*.

In the early days of my project on home, I called Victoria Moran, a New York writer who has written about what our souls need for a sense of home. I sensed that she and I occupied different wavelengths: she was the sort of person who could say "soul needs" without concern, whereas if I said it, I'd feel like an alien had taken over my body. But I liked Moran. She was smart, and when I asked why some places felt immediately like home, she said something that went straight to my gut.

"Sometimes we're lucky enough to come upon a place that's a teacher. That place might already nurture us in terms of its architecture and size and shape and design."

Our call went on from there – I asked whether dogs could help with home, and she immediately said yes – "They're love in a dog suit!" – but afterwards, what I thought about most often was her description of houses as teachers.

At the time, I'd written the phrase down and stared at it. Now, as I thought about the Newfoundland house, I rewrote it and understood it more fully. If my learned model of place was that it disappears, and takes people along with it, the house was teaching me something else, something about staying. It was replacing old ideas with new ones: about loss giving way to permanence, unpredictability giving way to stability, uncertainty giving way to security.

The house, of course, had been lost in the separation, but it was still there, still staring out at me from my computer screen. It was living up to what it had promised; it hadn't gone away.

As I said, I'm not normally a soul-needs, sage-burning sort of girl. But I felt the need to make the house's presence a continued fact of my life. I had to *notice* it and keep reminding myself of its lessons when I felt older ideas coming to the fore.

So I decided to do something that Clare Cooper Marcus advises: if a place has been meaningful in your life, commemorate what it has offered by creating a shrine to it.

Right away, I started following Marcus's suggestions as closely as I could. I put a wooden book stand on top of a low bookcase and then fished out an aerial photo of the house. This had been taken years earlier, when a neighbour was hoping to build a new garage. I'd gone to the planning office in St. John's for more information about the garage, and the official had printed the photo he had on file to show me how close to the river it might be.

"Do you want to keep it?" he asked. "I can always print a new one."

"Sure," I said. I thought the aerial view was kind of neat, but otherwise I treated it lightly. I shoved it into my diary for 2009, not realizing that, several years later, the photo would be all I had.

It was enough. The photo showed the river, the deck where Hodge and I used to sit, and the roof of the house, all dark and square and steady.

Then I kept on with Marcus's advice, which was to decorate the photo with things you'd leave at a real shrine. I added some plastic beads I'd gotten at a Pride parade, thinking they created a rosary effect. Then I set out two hand-painted candlesticks from Laura and added three dried flowers I'd bought at a country market years before.

I stepped back to study my work. Aside from the fact that the Pride beads were bright pink, it looked appropriately shrine-like. But I decided that *shrine* was not exactly the right word, since shrines are about the past, and I needed something to point me forward. So I grabbed a cue card and with a black marker wrote, "This is not your past. This is your future."

I ran off to the kitchen and returned with a pack of matches. I struck the match, and the candlelight flamed. The beads caught the light and reflected it back, and all the muted, dancing colours made the room feel warmer. Maybe a bit, or a lot, like home.

CHAPTER THREE

Local Place

Finding Belonging through What You Value

ONE OF THE REASONS MOST often cited for our lack of belonging isn't the experience of loss but rather the collapse of "place-based communities" – or, in plain language, neighbourhoods. When I was growing up, there was a show on TV called *King of Kensington*, about a shopkeeper living in Toronto's Kensington Market. Each show started with scenes of the shopkeeper, played by Al Waxman, walking the streets and greeting everyone in sight. There was a lively bustle to the neighbourhood that was immediately appealing. The sidewalks were packed, not just with residents but with goods: racks of dresses, overflowing fruit stands, sacks of coffee. The King himself was often shown hugging people, or patting children on the head. In the scene I liked best, he smiles dutifully as a woman drapes him in a fabric sample. In the final shot, the King lifts his arm and waves at someone just off-screen, and the smile he gives suggests that it's someone he's known for years.

The King's signature wave and smile made their way into grade school pop culture, with my ten-year-old classmates and I rushing up to each other in the schoolyard and

shouting, "Well now! It's great seeing *you* today." We knew
it was a TV show, and we lived so far north that most of us
had never been to the Market, but the familiarity the show
depicted wasn't too unfamiliar to us.

My friends and I ran in and out of people's yards and
houses like we owned them. We did this even with people
who didn't have kids. In retrospect, this strikes me as
slightly strange. Why would my best friend Stacey and I
have been allowed to play in the Swintons' yard, when they
were fifty and childless? I guess we saw it as normal because
they did too: we were neighbourhood kids and they were
neighbourhood residents. It might have struck them as
stranger if we hadn't treated their turf as our own.

That neighbourhood, of course, came down with a wreck-
ing ball, but the desire for a sense of belonging to local place
still holds strong. When I was just starting to think about
the subject, a friend from Newfoundland came to town. We
were driving through the northern edge of my neighbourhood when she started naming some familiar landmarks.

"There's the school," she said, with a touch of nostalgia.

I couldn't understand why Allison, who'd left Toronto
twenty years earlier, knew the streets and schools in my area.

"Why is any of this familiar to you?" I asked.

She named an old girlfriend – Suzie – and said, "She
used to live around here. I remember picking her up, or
getting out at the subway and walking to her place. She was
Al Waxman's daughter. They had a big house around here."

I couldn't wrap my head around this.

"You mean Al Waxman lived up here?"

We were in the posh part of my neighbourhood, and Allison seemed to think I was surprised that an actor could afford an expensive home. She started explaining that Al Waxman had been quite successful, but I already knew this. I was confused about something else.

"You mean he *didn't* live in Kensington Market?"

We were at a stoplight. Allison swivelled to see if I was joking. I wasn't. She cracked up.

"Of course he didn't live there. It was a TV show."

I slumped in my seat, awash with disbelief. I guess I'd never really thought about it until that moment, but if you'd asked me even five minutes earlier where Al Waxman had lived, I would have said, "Kensington Market." It was like I needed to believe in what the show offered: the vision of the King walking out his door and knowing everyone in sight.

Marketers know we want this. I read the "New in Homes" section of the newspaper faithfully, even though I have no interest in new homes. What I love are the ads, with their open emphasis on belonging and connection. I clipped out a ten-line ad for a new subdivision because it was so shameless in this respect, offering up variations on the words *community* and *belonging* fourteen times. The ad even featured its own narrative arc. Belonging was first cast as something we've lost – "Remember an era when neighbours were friends and looked after each other?" – and then as something we can recover: "Our community has been planned to make this way of life possible again."

I like the housing ads because they make me feel smart. (I know this is setting the bar pretty low, but I take my affirmations where I find them.) The corny drawings of sunlit homes, the smiling families, the gleeful dogs leaping for endless Frisbees – I always feel like it's a game in which I'm catching the marketers out before they catch me.

But I'm not sure, looking back, who was really winning this game. Because when I started thinking about local place, my thinking wasn't too far off from what the ads promised. I wanted a quick fix – something I didn't have to work too hard for – and deep down I believed that if I just found the right setting, belonging would wash over me like water in a bath.

Granted, my vision of the right setting differed from the ones in the papers. I didn't want prefab housing in a depleted soy field. I wanted a tight-knit neighbourhood filled with organic gardens, hand-painted hydro poles, wacky deck furniture, windows full of dream catchers, and at least one house featuring rows of wild corn where the grass should be.

I'd lived in such a neighbourhood in my thirties – it was and is called Riverdale. I arranged to meet Chris there one afternoon in early spring. She had a doctor's appointment nearby, and I wanted to pick up fish oil at the local holistic dispensary. Before meeting her, I took a walk and tried to understand why I loved the neighbourhood so much. Part of it had to do with what my Newfoundland house had offered: the neighbourhood felt stable, like it wasn't going anywhere. Aside from paint jobs and some front porch renovations, the houses looked mostly unchanged from when they'd been built eighty years before. Many people in Toronto pave their front yards to create parking spaces, but very few Riverdale residents had done so. This meant there was more greenery, and the greenery made the area feel lush. The roads were all one-way; hills gave the area character; even the cat I saw crossing the street looked fluffier than the cats in my own neighbourhood.

The coffee shop Chris had chosen was tucked between the dispensary and an indie bookstore, and it was filled to the brim with people working on laptops, reading the paper, or chatting quietly. The café was warm and smelled of baked goods, and the windows were steamed up against the cold outside. The sheer coziness, combined with the peace and stability I'd just seen outside, filled me with longing. *If only I lived here*, I thought, *belonging would present itself in an instant.*

Chris broke this reverie by telling me that I might want to find a table. She had a cup of tea in hand and was trying to get the barista's attention.

"You probably want to sit down," she said. "I have to be Mom for a second."

My mother is well known in my family for restaurant requests. Could she get her beer in a wine glass? Could they turn down the music? Would it be possible to get her coffee reheated? My sisters and I all cringe when she does this but then go on to do it ourselves. Chris, at that moment, was asking the barista to fill her cup to the brim.

"They think you're going to add milk or something," she said to me, half irritably, half apologetically. "But I'm not, so there's too much empty space."

"I would have done the same thing," I said.

"How's the new place?" Chris and I were now settled into armchairs that were pushed close together. I briefly wondered when and why living room furniture had entered coffee shops. Straight-back chairs are an awful lot more practical. Chris and I had to sit at the edge of our cushions to hear each other.

"Better," I said. This was true. After creating the shrine to my Newfoundland home – and then following Clare Cooper Marcus's instructions to talk to it every day – my anxiety levels had dropped. I was still working on "beauti-fying" my home, but I no longer felt, when carrying home a vase, that I was clutching a time bomb. "I just wish the neighbourhood was different."

"What's wrong with the neighbourhood? Isn't it a lot like here?"

I was amazed at how wrong she could be. She knew my neighbourhood. We lived in the same city. I let out a little hoot of disbelief.

"It is totally *not* like here."

"It was built around the same time." Chris, now a suc-cessful tech exec, was married to an architect, and she noticed these things. I'd noticed too. My north-end flat was in a house of pretty much the same style that my house in Riverdale had been – meaning that what had struck me as old and quirky was really the cookie-cutter subdivision of 1928.

"Still, it's . . . it's different."

"The streets are nice."

"The streets are *crazy*." This was true. Condos were going in where smaller shops and old houses had been, meaning that whole blocks were covered with hoardings, and giant dust clouds rose up whenever the wind hit. There was an abandoned bus bay at the main intersection that looked post-apocalyptic with its dangling signs and pavement overgrown with weeds; the main drag was filled with corporate storefronts; the subway station felt like a cattle chute; and at lunchtime, two high schools disgorged so many teens that you could barely get down the sidewalk.

"I mean," I said, "you're basically taking your life in your hands every time you cross the street."

Chris smiled. A tendency toward emotional overstatement runs strong in both of us, and in Terri too. We can all be a bit theatrical, rolling our eyes at lineups, or throwing our hands in the air, or sighing too loudly when irritated. I see it as the flip side of our high pain threshold. Fly off a bike into the curb? No problem. Wait three minutes behind someone asking for a price check? Completely lose it. Right then, I had my elbows on the table and my hands clenched under my chin, like I was furiously praying.

"I'm sure you'll find a way to feel comfortable there," Chris said, in the low-pitched voice we all use on each other at times like this.

I checked myself emotionally. She was right: crossing the street didn't *always* mean taking my life in my hands. But I wasn't sure I'd find a way to feel comfortable. I hadn't told her about the main problem, which was that I didn't seem to *match* with anyone around me there.

I'd tried. I'd signed up for an aquafit class at the local rec centre. One thing I was willing to concede was that my neighbourhood community centre rocked. Architecturally, it bordered on Rich Person's Cottage, with lots of exposed beams and natural light. And I liked how accessible it was, with cheap classes, pool lifts for the disabled, and plenty of space for just hanging out. The desk where I picked up my aquafit ticket was surrounded by tables, and these were filled with teens eating lunch, elderly men staring at newspapers, and ten-year-olds playing ping-pong. This was diversity, and I *valued* diversity – or at least, I valued it in theory.

When it came to diversity in practice, I was a bit less enthusiastic. It's not that I didn't like my aquafit class. I actually kind of loved it. It was led by an eighty-year-old man in a skin-tight leotard who did movements on the pool deck while we did them in the water. We walked up the shallow end of the pool, waving our arms in the air, then walked back down, our arms still swinging. Fred Astaire played on the tape deck, and a lot of the time all we did was bounce. I loved the sight of the dark night beyond the pool windows, and the unruffled surface of the deep end, and the luxurious sense of having the whole place to ourselves. My classmates – most of them plump women in floral swimsuits and older men in shorts so long they seemed designed to maximize drag – seemed similarly relaxed by the whole scene, and when the class ended, more than one came round to extend a welcome.

"You look like you can swim," one woman said

approvingly. She was stout but solid, and wearing a skirted swimsuit so pretty it wouldn't have been out of place at a cocktail party.

My racerback Speedo was clearly marking me out as sporty. "I can," I admitted. Everyone was looking for their flip-flops, and I was trying to work my feet into a pair of Crocs before anyone saw my toes.

"There's a harder class on Wednesday," the woman told me. "Or you can keep coming here. I know it's not much of a workout," she added, glancing at the instructor and lowering her voice, "but sometimes that can be nice."

"It can be," I said, agreeing completely. And as the clutch of older women and I headed toward the change room, our voices bouncing off the walls, I felt warmed, both by the gentle class itself and by the easy camaraderie.

But I didn't go back, and that's because none of the people at the class were like me. This sounds shallow, or like an extension of my own private fondness for matching, but it's actually an important principle that guides our behaviour more than we think. Some of the key items on the Neighbourhood Sense of Community Scale created by Ohio State University sociologists Jack Nasar and David Julian have to do with how much the people in your neighbourhood are like you, such as, "I am quite similar to most people who live here," and, "Being a member of this neighbourhood is like being a member of a group of friends." The more you can agree with these statements – at least, according to the logic of the scale – the more belonging you'll feel in local place.

More and more of us are acting on this principle. What experts refer to as *sorting*, especially in relation to neighbourhoods, is becoming more pronounced as other ways of belonging begin to recede. People who have the money are willing to spend it on homes in places where they look and act like the people they see around them – people who might drive hybrid cars, set out woodsy porch furniture, or name their kids after water formations. There's nothing really wrong with this, but it does give rise to some issues. The first is that the sorting that occurs locally can start to feel necessary in all other settings, so you wind up with a sorted book group, a sorted prayer circle, and a meditation class where everyone looks and tends to think just like you. More significantly, sorting blinds us to what belonging is really about. Since we feel we "fit" in a neighbourhood (or book group or prayer circle) where everyone is just like us, we start to think it's the similarity that's cuing belonging. It's not. The similarity is shorthand for something else, but the more we sort, the less likely we are to realize this.

I certainly didn't realize it at first. I was convinced that if I couldn't find a local place where people were willing to play farmer in their tiny front yards or hang mounted deer heads ironically upside down, I just would never belong at all.

It was my friend Ron who set me straight. I met Ron in 1995, when I sublet a room for the summer from his regular roommate. When I moved in, I thought he was odd. He was finishing a Ph.D., and he wrote at night instead of during the day. This meant I'd come home from work to find him just rolling out of bed. It was strange to be sharing a kitchen with a large man in a blue bathrobe making toast at six at night, but as we took to eating dinner/breakfast together, I realized there was something special about him. He seemed able to see right through me, but he always presented his observations neutrally, without judgment and without any suggestion that he had anything particularly insightful to say. I later realized he was deeply religious and that he set kindness and humility as personal goals, but that summer I was just amazed to meet this huge guy – Ron was six foot two and barrel-chested – who was as sensitive as Oprah.

When he heard me, eighteen years later, complaining about my neighbourhood, he brought his usual intelligence and compassion to bear on my situation, agreeing that it was hard to feel like you didn't belong. But he also seemed amused by something. Ron was the child of immigrants who had never learned to speak English, and he'd put himself through two degrees by working construction. Although he never said so, I think he saw me as soft.

"The area's not exactly working-class," he said with a slight grin.

I was taken aback. I hadn't used the word *class* at all.

"I know it's not working-class," I replied. It wasn't. Maps of Toronto that break down neighbourhoods by income show most of the downtown core as bright red, with people earning, on average, $88,000 a year or more. My own area was one of only two downtown that were still orange, meaning that individual incomes were around $39,000. Incomes were lower around me because the big apartment buildings that had gone up in the neighbourhood in the 1960s and 1970s still charged reasonable rents. The buildings were well maintained, but they managed to communicate a sense of both upward and downward mobility: some residents were just putting in time until they could afford to move to a red neighbourhood, while others were trying to avoid relocating to a yellow one (where average incomes start at zero and usually don't go above $27,000).

I knew that tenants usually felt less place connection than homeowners, but I'd been a tenant for years in Riverdale and had loved the place, so ownership couldn't be the main issue.

"It's not class," I continued. "It's that it's not . . ." I ran into the difficulty I'd faced with Chris. I couldn't name the problem. The neighbourhood wasn't *what*?

"Rich?" Ron suggested, with the same sneaky smile. Years after I had a sublet a room in his apartment, he had sublet from me, so he'd spent a year in my Riverdale flat. He knew the area as well as I did – the lush lawns, the old trees, the fluffy cats.

"Because if that's what you want," he was saying, "it's going to be kind of hard to repeat now." He didn't say, *Because you're no longer a lawyer*, but I took his point. We were sitting in plastic chairs in the sort of coffee shop so unambitious you'd never describe it as a café. People all around us were having loud conversations while drinking coffee out of paper cups and eating chili out of plastic bowls. Aside from the acidic coffee-chili aroma, I didn't really mind the place. I had, after all, been raised by two

Depression-era parents. While they'd both gone on to earn good incomes, they had never seen themselves as rich. My dad, in particular, never missed an opportunity to tell me that my "people" – my aunts and cousins down south – didn't have much money at all. If he had heard me say that I needed a posh neighbourhood in order to belong, he would have been appalled.

I looked at Ron. I'd noticed a long time ago how much he resembled my dad – same height, same dark hair, same bookishness, same humility. Ron didn't take my hand and say, *Dear heart, that's not the way you were raised*, but he might as well have.

I thought of Hagerty's Rule – you need a sense of fit in order to belong – and decided I didn't want a sense of belonging that was predicated on being loaded. I hadn't forgotten the lesson I'd learned at yoga: if you're buying belonging, you can lose it if your income drops. This was actually what had happened to me with Riverdale. I loved the place, but I couldn't afford to move back in.

This meant I had to find a way of belonging that had nothing to do with either matching or paying. Helpfully, I didn't have to start from scratch. There are loads of place researchers who offer up some very practical suggestions about how to connect to a sense of neighbourhood. Unlike the popular advice on home decor, with its nebulous emphasis on colour and light, I found these tips easy to relate to. There was no element of fantasy to what the place researchers were saying – no claw-foot tubs filled with gardenia blossoms – and not a word about money.

A lot of the advice had to do with "the concentration of daily routines," meaning doing everything you need to do locally. But I was already doing this without much discernable effect. (What the researchers don't note is that you need to do this over a *long* period of time, like a year. A month-long immersion project might prove interesting, but it won't create place belonging, because you'll be thinking of all the neat places you'll be able to go once the month is over.) I found "studying local history" – another recommendation – enjoyable. I particularly loved the photos of aproned shopkeepers standing with their arms crossed in the doorways of buildings I still recognized. But I found I worried too much about the horses – in every single photo, they seemed to be knee-deep in mud – and pictures of the past had the inevitable effect of reminding me that big chunks of this past were being gutted as condos went in. I tried to create "stimulus shelters" – areas in my neighbourhood that felt uniquely peaceful – but I kept forgetting that I had them. I'd walk past my quiet spot in the cemetery only to realize, five minutes later, that I had missed it *again*.

I finally decided I wasn't setting my sights high enough. The gold standard for local belonging is the "great good place." You can think of the great good place in terms of specific criteria – you feel comfortable walking in alone, you're made to feel welcome, the ties you make there rarely extend beyond the place itself – or you can just sum it up as the bar on *Cheers*, the place "where everybody knows your name."

The sociologist Ray Oldenburg, who coined the term

"great good place," devoted a whole book to how we're losing such places, and how their loss leaves us with less of a sense of connection. Having read Oldenburg's book, I knew that what I was looking for amounted to one of my beloved endangered species – something that still existed but was much harder to find. Coffee shops are often held out as potential great good places, but few of my local coffee shops had that "sit a spell" feel to them: most were franchises clustered around the subway station and catering to people in a rush. So I switched to the library, a truly wonderful spot with big windows and a boisterous children's reading room, and tried to strike up a conversation with a woman in the Staff Picks section. This woman, who was short and very tidy looking, with a pixie cut, had a novel called *State of Wonder* in her hand.

"I loved that," I said eagerly, pointing to the book.

The woman seemed a bit startled to find herself talking to a stranger, but her manners quickly recovered.

"I've never read" – she paused to read the author's name – "Ann Patchett."

I'd read a lot of Ann Patchett, and I saw this as an entry point.

"She's got this novel called *Bel Canto*," I said enthusiastically. "It's about this opera singer who gets kidnapped – well, a whole bunch of people get kidnapped – and they're in South America—" Then I stopped, because I realized this might not be the woman's thing at all. What if she was a Stieg Larsson type, hungry for murderous Nordic psychopaths? I pulled back.

"It's really good," I concluded. It wasn't clear, even to me, which novel I was referring to at this point. The woman was still smiling politely, and we sort of bowed at each other before I headed off to Non-fiction. I knew I'd just proved one of Oldenburg's main points: even if we're lucky enough to live near a well-functioning local place, we no longer expect anyone in that place to talk to us.

Back at home, I looked at my list of local belongingness projects. I'd crossed off "immersion project," "stimulus shelters," and "local history." It seemed like I was going to have to cross "great good place" off the list as well. But then I started thinking about what was happening at the local pool. I'd given up on aquafit, but I was still swimming most days. The pool was the one place in my neighbour-hood where I did feel a sense of connection. I love to swim, and the place reminded me of the community pool where Stacey and I used to spend weekends in our old neighbour-hood. Chlorine smells good to me, because it brings with it memories of Stacey doing cannonballs and daring me to do bellyflops.

I wasn't, of course, still doing those things (though part of me longed to). My routine was more sedate. I did the front crawl for forty-five minutes every other day. But this was getting boring, so I decided to shake things up and try water-walking. This involved wrapping an orange flotation device around my waist and wading into the only lane where walking was possible: the "social" lane.

I didn't really know what went on in the social lane. Without my glasses, I couldn't see it from my usual spot in the fast lane. From what I could make out, activity there seemed to involve elderly men and women floating around on water wings. I wasn't expecting anything to happen when I got there. I certainly wasn't expecting anyone to know my name.

I apologized when I saw a woman with hair the colour of new pennies bobbing toward me.

"You can let me know if I get in your way," I said. "I can't see you very well."

"That's okay, Emma," the copper-headed woman said.

I was baffled. "How did you know my name?"

"You mean we got it *right*?" she shrieked. She called to another woman – bleached blonde – doing push-ups against the side of the pool. "Susan, we got it *right*."

It took me some time to sort out what was happening. The social lane regulars had names for the regulars in the other lanes. ("Everyone?" I asked. "Just the ones who interest us," Copper replied.) The ones who interested them were named after movie stars, and I was Emma Thompson. I felt flattered but also vaguely lost, because I realized the names were part of a different way of speaking that existed only in the social lane.

First of all, the social lane wasn't the social lane: it was the "dolphin pod," or just "the pod," which explained statements I'd heard in the change room but had never understood. The kids on the deck were "the little bastards." The elderly man who approached the pool with trembling knees was "Trouble." There were unspoken rules about conversation – food was discussed most of all (I once paddled through a whole discussion about white balsamic vinegar), followed by grandkids and medication. "I'm on Zoloft," I heard one man tell another, as they both floated, "but I think this place helps more than anything." There were also rules about what Copper referred to as "not working too hard."

I was still doing my little laps.

"Is this working too hard?" I asked Copper one afternoon in late April.

"It's close," she replied. She had never properly introduced herself, and I had noticed that she had a tendency toward obliqueness, answering every question in a way that made me want to ask another question.

After about three weeks, it became clear that the men and women who knew each other so well in the pod – and who called out such warm greetings as they saw each other arrive – didn't socialize outside of it. Whole dinner parties were planned without any expectation that the people listening would be invited. At home, after my failed library venture, I thought about Oldenburg's criteria for great good places and realized that I could tick off every box for the pool: people arrived solo; they found companionship in an accessible place; and companionship was confined to that place. It was that rare thing, the endangered pine marten of the social world, an honest-to-God great good place. And I knew I was being accepted as part of the pod when people began making jokes about me.

"Dear," Copper teased one sunny afternoon, "you're so blind you should be swimming with a cane."

Belonging was right in front of me. It was like staring at a high-quality street drug. I'd found the purest possible form of local connection, but some part of me didn't want to take it.

"And it's not the age thing," I said. I'd invited Laura back over to show her some of my apartment improvements. She particularly liked the small rosewood table that had precipitated my panic about causing road accidents. Right then, we were in the kitchen. I'd put a blue placemat in the centre of the table to add the colour she'd suggested. She was toying with one of the apples that sat in the silver mixing bowl on top.

"It's more like . . ." I paused. I often waited for Laura to finish my sentences. I'd flag a problem and then let her sort it out. This habit had begun in law school and had just expanded, possibly without her even noticing, to encompass my whole life.

"It's not the age that matters," she said, launching into the explanation I was looking for. "It's the social skills. People our age don't know how to behave like that anymore."

She sounded a bit mournful, and she picked an apple out of the bowl to consider it more closely. Laura had grown up attending church socials with people much older than herself. As a ten-year-old, she'd been passing around iced tea to women in their eighties. Even with the addition of new makeup and tighter tops, Laura still didn't seem quite modern. With her hair pulled back, it was easy to imagine her in an ankle-length skirt, boiling up pots of stew for barn-raisings or talking to her hens. When she discussed our generation, the "our" part always sounded slightly forced, as if she didn't really see herself as a member of the group she was describing.

"We want everything to be really unfixed today. We don't like the notion of strangers knowing us. Or, if they do know us, we want to be able to walk away."

"You know, that's it. I feel sort of hemmed in. Like I *have* to show up."

"Well, you do. That's part of what being in a group is all about. It's showing up."

"But I don't like people expecting me to be there. Or having to talk when I don't feel like talking."

"That's the modern part. We want groups to be there when we need them. We want people to talk to when we need them. But we want all of that to be on our own terms. So we don't go, or we don't talk. And then we say we don't have enough groups."

"Are you part of anything like that?" I asked. "Where you go even if you don't feel like socializing?"

"My Amnesty group. But it's only once a month, and we're writing letters. What you're describing sounds way more social. I might not be comfortable with it, either," she concluded, sounding a bit wistful.

Having Laura – sweet, socially skilled Laura – say that the group might be too much for her felt like permission for me to leave it. But leaving was more awkward than I'd thought it would be. I started going a bit later, since most of the pod people got there for noon, when lane swim began, but there were always some stragglers who'd wave if I walked in at one o'clock. Worse, appearing late meant

I'd run into some of the pod women, including Copper, in the change room, where I'd be partly or completely naked. Grabbing a towel while being asked, "Hey, where have you been?" was excruciating.

I wasn't sure of what to do until a cat solved the problem for me. Hodge and I were house-sitting for my mother when her Siamese went into attack mode. My choices were clear: grab my mom's cat, or watch Hodgie die. It was a non-decision. I pulled Remy off the ground and stood frozen as he tore his nails through my palms and bit my arm so hard he hit bone. I showed up at the ER five days later, my lower arm as big as a balloon, and watched the doctor slice open the bites. I couldn't feel anything – the whole area was anaesthetized – and I might have been slightly in shock, because all I could think as I watched the blood geyser out was, *Well, I guess I won't be back in the pool any time soon.*

Bandaged, I decided that I'd sort of liked the feel of a great good place: having a local spot where I was known did help with feelings of belonging. But the dolphin pod was the wrong fit. While some people might love a local place filled with conversation, I needed a place where I'd be welcomed and recognized without feeling like I had to show up every single week, or that I had to talk when I did show up.

It was in this state of mind – I was actually staring in at the pool from the ground-level windows – that I turned around and saw a sign saying that "worker bees" were needed for a community garden. The garden was right beside the pool – set off by just a footpath – and I'd already stopped there a few times to admire the soil beds awaiting planting and the tidy rows of saplings. The strange thing about the garden was that I'd never seen anyone in it. It was as if it were tended by sprites in the night. But the sign said that real humans appeared every Wednesday at five, so I made the decision to go.

I arrived the following Wednesday to find a whole hive of people. I wondered how it was possible that I'd never noticed any of them, and whether there had been other connection opportunities I'd missed simply because I hadn't been paying enough attention. Still feeling a bit surprised, I started trying to find the group leader. An older woman in gardening gloves and a Tilley hat said the leader's name was Heidi, and she pointed to a glamorous blonde in a cowboy hat and tight white top. I started to follow Heidi as she, in turn, followed an irrigation repairman. A vandal had cut several lengths of hose, and Heidi was trying to oversee volunteers while keeping up a running dialogue with the workman. I stood beside her as the workman outlined options, all of which sounded expensive, since they involved running new lines in from the rec centre.

"Is there a way to just patch them?" Heidi asked. Then she turned to me and said, "Oh, hi. Did you email?"

I felt a bit sheepish. "I thought you could just show up."

The irrigation man was now watching the two of us.

"You can! You can!" Heidi said, sounding a bit scattered. "But can you just wait a sec?"

I said I could. I walked to the hill beside the garden and surveyed the activity. There was a clutch of twenty-somethings beside an asparagus bed, and I heard the word

asparagus repeated so many times, and in so many different accents, that I figured (correctly) it was an ESL conversation group. One young man was using a pitchfork to
move soil between bins, another was pruning raspberry
bushes, and the Tilley-hatted woman who'd greeted me
was telling a teenage girl to keep watering the saplings
with a jug – it was going to be a hot summer, and they
needed all the water they could get.

Maybe it was the fact that the garden was out in the
sunshine, or that so much was happening at once, but I
began to feel very much at home. I was surprised that so
many of the worker bees were younger than me: somehow,
I'd thought the volunteers would *all* be Tilley-hatted fifty-
year-olds. I wasn't sure my fellow volunteers matched with
me – the ESL students were recent immigrants, and the
bearded young guys looked hipper than me – but there was
something about these people, or about the activity itself,
that felt like a good fit.

My spot on the hill also gave me a great view of the park
as a whole. It was six blocks long and three blocks wide, but
it didn't feel like a big open space. In most spots, it felt like
a series of semi-connected pieces. There was the shady,
more heavily treed area higher up the hill – a place where
teens sat in groups and older men sat alone on benches;
beyond that, the hill dipped down to the garden; then it
dipped even lower to a dog-walking area where people
stood chatting as their pets raced around. Then, if you kept
walking north, you hit a baseball diamond, a playground,
another dog park, and a soccer field.

It certainly didn't feel bad to walk through the park and experience it in pieces, but it felt even better to do what I'd never done before: pick a spot with a good view and absorb the park as a whole. There was something kinder about it when viewed this way. People no longer seemed separated into groups, with the little kids in one area and the baseball players in another. Everyone looked like they were together, and suddenly, since I was about to be assigned a role in the park, that togetherness included me too.

When the workman finally reached for his cellphone, I saw my chance to firm up my insider status and get Heidi's attention.

"Hi," I said again, popping up behind her.

"Oh, have you been waiting long?" She had clearly forgotten about me but was trying to hide this.

"Not too long. Can I help?"

She looked at my bandaged hand and then at the garden. Most of the tasks seemed to be claimed, but then she pointed to the garden's sign.

"Can you paint?" she asked.

This seemed like an unusual question to get at a garden, but I said I sort of could.

"Great," she said, sounding relieved. "No one wants to paint."

She led me to a wooden bench covered in backpacks and reached underneath for a plastic bag. She pulled out an impressive assortment of brushes and paints, then handed me a yogurt tub ("for water") and a Frisbee ("for your palette").

"The sign is completely fading," she continued. The

prospect of painting the garden's main sign – the one with block letters welcoming passersby – seemed like an important job. I was surprised to get it. I was even more surprised by how hard I started to work. I was using bright white paint, and I wanted every letter to look perfect. I used my fingers to wipe off any paint that fell on the backdrop, and I covered the same letters over and over again to make them vivid. This wasn't just my usual obsessiveness coming to the fore. I was proud of the sign – maybe a bit proud of the garden – and I wanted this pride to show.

There was a composting session being held beside me, and I listened to worm trivia as I zeroed in on the letters. (I learned that worms do eat meat, but they also breathe through their skin, so if you put too much meat in a composter, the grease will suffocate them.) The worm lessons were interesting, and the sign was looking great. I didn't want to stop, but when another worker bee arrived two hours later and asked if she could help, I had to admit I was starving.

"Try to keep the paint really neat," I said, imposing the perfectionism Heidi hadn't imposed on me. Then I walked back through the garden to find Heidi sitting on one of the benches, sifting through a binder.

"You headed out?" she asked. Her cowboy hat and tight clothes gave her a hint of Daisy Duke. I was a bit in awe of her – not just her looks, but her easy way of making people feel welcome. There were no forms, no membership fees, just her dimpled smile and her cheerful expectation of seeing me again.

I said I was.

"Till next week, then," she said, touching the tip of her hat in a sort of salute.

I tapped my own forehead to return the salute, then headed into the park. The sun was starting to dip below the hill, creating a patch of shadow that stretched across the garden but left the rest of the park in full light. I'd gotten used to the shade, but as I headed down the hill, the sun hit me once again. The lawn had been cut that morning, and the air felt thick, like the grass was breathing. Dogs were running past, their owners laughing about something, and I started to think that maybe I'd been wrong, that maybe what I needed for belonging was right there – all around me and right under my feet.

When I got home, I went to the kitchen table to write the date of the next worker bee session in my "place" file. As I did so, I noticed the edge of a map I'd drawn a few months earlier.

It was what I called my "connection map." I'd created it after reading the work of British psychologist David Canter. Canter had noticed that, when he asked people in a single neighbourhood to map that neighbourhood, everyone drew a different map. Some maps were social – filled with houses and apartments of friends and family members – while others were "behavioural," filled with shops and offices that people found useful. Canter believed that a quickly drawn sketch could reveal how someone *thought* about their neighbourhood; it was an external representation of what was going on in their heads.

Canter made it clear that you could map anything, and since I was interested in connection, I'd decided to map that. A few months before, I had followed Canter's instructions – don't think, just draw – and tried to map where I felt connected. I'd seen the result as proof that connection didn't exist. I'd drawn the park, then the road that served as a link between the park and the dog run six blocks away, then the walking trail and the cemetery that sat beside it. "Empty space," I'd written, frustrated there was nothing to belong to.

That June morning, as I looked at the map again, I realized I *had* mapped connection. Every place on my map was either a green space or a link to a green space. I added the garden to the map – sketching it in at the edge of the park – and realized that all the places I'd drawn could be grouped under the heading of "nature."

Nature was something I valued. This, of course, was not a surprise. I had, after all, been a professional tree hugger. What surprised me was the fact that I hadn't paid attention to this value presenting itself in plain form. When I thought about belonging, I pictured Riverdale, where my neighbours had grown native grasses in their yards and looked after new trees like babies. (One of these neighbours had named the sapling beside her sidewalk "Albert" and hosted Albert Watering Days.) My environmental values hadn't stood out there because everyone shared them, and the fact that everyone shared them made me feel like I fit in.

In my new neighbourhood, I saw paved yards, dump trucks, overcrowded streets, and the abandoned bus bay. It wasn't just that the main parts of the 'hood weren't green; it was that the lack of greenery made it seem like no one cared about the same things I did.

And maybe a lot of the people I saw on the streets really didn't care – or they cared about other things. But that didn't mean there weren't *some* people who cared. I just had to put some effort into finding them. The fact that finding them hadn't been immediate or easy made me realize that I'd been looking for a shortcut. When I said I wanted others to "be like me," what I really wanted was a sense of shared values. That's what a lot of us are looking for when it comes to belonging. We're not wrong in wanting it; a sense of shared values is probably a pre-condition for fitting in. What's wrong is thinking that this commonality has to be visible, or total, or already in place. That's what sorted neighbourhoods do: they announce what's valued – be it pickup trucks or expensive strollers or posters for fetish parties – and in this way communicate what's important to that community and who should or should not view themselves as a member.

But you can create your own sense of membership by focusing on whatever it is you value. I created a little equation in my head that said, "connection = green," and then I went after it.

I volunteered at the garden every week. Showing up never made me feel hemmed in or forced, because I wanted to be there and I always had something to do. Experts who write about local place stress that touch can help with connection, and while this seemed strange to me in theory, it felt amazing in practice. I came to love sinking my fingers into the dry, heated soil during the course of what became a hot summer; pulling at chunks of grass and watching the white roots appear, all slender, with tiny insects scrambling to get back to the darkness; and hosing down the vegetable bed, feeling the water start to seep around the edges of my sandals.

Even times when nothing much was happening were good. One night, about seven weeks in, I arrived to realize there was a vermicomposting lecture scheduled. Heidi herded most of us over to listen to a man talk about punching air holes into plastic bins. I was looking for an escape route – either back home or to the other side of the garden, where some nonconformists were stealthily tying up tomato plants – but then Heidi sat down beside me, and I realized I was trapped. So I gave in. As the vermicomposting expert talked about freezing worm eggs, I stretched out on the concrete riser we were sitting on. The concrete was warm, and the riser was right beside the flower bed. Lying down brought me eye to eye with black-eyed Susans, whose yellow-and-black colour scheme was mirrored by the bees circling round. I stared at the flowers as Heidi began tapping my sandals with a twig. The soil beside me smelled like wild carrot, and I finally closed my eyes, breathing deeply and thinking I could stay on that riser for hours. "Auction," I eventually heard someone say, and I hauled myself up to watch people I'd come to know and like cheer each other on as a lucky few won worm bins.

While I ultimately did find a second great good place in this challenge, the garden became one in the truest sense, because it was local. It was straight from *King of Kensington*: all I had to do was walk out my door, and a group of people would greet me and wave. And the best part about it was that I could show up and not *do* much. The whole task for an evening might be devising a way of keeping rats out of a tomato bed. This would involve me and another volunteer passing plastic netting back and forth, saying things like, "Well, if we string it overtop, the plants can't grow," or "If we tuck it into the soil, won't the rats just burrow underneath?" Our conversation would ramble, and as it went on we would slowly pick all the baby tomatoes off the stalks and eat them, inadvertently solving the rat problem by beating them to the food.

In an era where we're supposed to be constantly busy, and where this busyness has leached into our social lives, such drifting was wonderfully freeing. It was reassuring in a way we've lost sight of. Ray Oldenburg notes that one thing great good places provide is "a little time off." The place itself is grounding, and the relationships are warm but undemanding. Oldenburg argues, quite seriously, that tranquilizer use has risen in tandem with local places disappearing. It was a point the older man in the dolphin pod had made openly – that casual socializing helped his depression much more than his meds did.

And the feeling of not being asked for much can signal its own sort of commitment. Just because the ties are light doesn't mean they're not strong. In late September, as the garden was winding down, Heidi arranged to have the leader of another garden come in to teach us how to build small greenhouses. The instructor arrived late – there'd been a problem with the door at her underground garage – and she was clearly not what Heidi was expecting. Everything about her was circular: she wore a big sunhat, hoop earrings, and a sundress clinched by a big belt around her middle. I hadn't realized how low-key our garden was until this woman swung into action, pelting us with questions.

"Who knows the difference between an annual and a perennial?" she asked. There were twelve of us sitting in a circle around her. We looked at each other blankly. We all knew the difference.

"One requires replanting and the other can survive the winter to bloom again in the spring," Maureen – my neighbour in the Tilley hat – politely explained.

"Excellent! You guys are going to *rock* at this!"

It was too much. Everything was overexplained. The instructor was surrounded by boxes she'd hauled from her car, and she started passing sheets of plastic around so that we could all experience what six millimetres of plastic sheeting really felt like.

I handed a sheet to Heidi, who caught my eye and winced. If the whole evening was going to play out like this, her look suggested, it was going to be a long night.

It was. The instructor's late arrival had set us back, and since it was starting to border on fall, the sun was setting early. The hill behind us created a shadow of its own, and by seven-thirty it was nearly dark. Heidi, good sport that she was, pulled on a sort of midnight gardening cap, with a bright light fixed in the middle of a headband; others, like

Maureen, pulled out smartphones to shine them on the instructor, who was jumping from the risks posed by *E. coli* to the types of wrapping you need to keep frost off plants. It was getting cold, but none of us moved. If we left, it would be a signal to Heidi that she'd misjudged, and none of us wanted her to feel that way.

So we ended up being there until nine at night. Heidi kept her gardening light on, but everyone else quietly switched off their phones. We were back to what we did best: sitting together, not doing much. Some walkers were still out with their dogs; I could hear barking in the distance. I was only half-listening to the presenter. I pulled at the grass and realized how at home I felt. It was a funny sort of belonging. I was in the dark, and shivering, but I was happy. In fact, I was probably happier than I'd ever been in Riverdale, where belonging had been served up so easily. Here, I'd had to make it happen. The process hadn't been easy, but it had led to scenes like these, with me leaning over to whisper to Heidi, her miner's light making her hair glow blonde, and quietly asking if I could, when we were finished, maybe take a squash or two. They were big that year, and I'd heard they were sweet.

CHAPTER FOUR

Caring

How to Belong Even When You're Told You Probably Shouldn't

A BIG PART OF CONNECTING to my neighbourhood was recognizing how much I valued the green spaces, and one of the things I valued about the green spaces was that there were so many dogs in them. The two parks nearest me were filled with chihuahuas, Great Danes, and just about every breed and size in between. There were dogs I saw so often that I came to think of them as "mine": the stout and calm Jack Russell who seemed oddly indifferent to other dogs, the collie who'd circle around me before racing off toward someone more interesting, the rescued greyhound who was allowed to run off leash on the hill beside the garden. Whenever this happened, someone would shout, "Look!" and we'd all stop and stare as the dog sailed across the ground like her body was the wind.

The dogs always made me feel good; even if I was deep in ruminations about my ex-girlfriend, the sight of a terrier's bright eyes and shaggy bangs would lift my spirits and take me out of myself. They were like little meditation instructors – four-legged reminders to Be Here Now – and their cheerful expressions always made me search for some similar cheer in myself.

It was, however, only the dogs I was seeing in person that had this effect on me. Dogs in the news were an entirely different matter. I've come to think that if you're a dog, you probably don't want to wind up in a headline, because it often runs like this: HUMANE SOCIETY INVESTIGATION TRACES EXPENSIVE PUPS TO PUPPY MILLS.

Stories like this made my stress levels soar. I'd force myself to start reading the article, but I would choke on the first line: "Living in filth and lacking basic care, 121 dogs were rescued from a puppy mill in Jefferson County, Arkansas." The photo would be even worse: a pup hobbled outside a wet plastic tent, its eyes unable to focus and its fur so matted it looked rubbed down with dirt. And I wouldn't be able to get any further. Something like fear would rise up in me, and I'd have to click away from the story and distract myself with something else: weather reports, sports news, articles about gridlock that didn't affect me since I don't own a car.

My goal was always to make myself not feel anything, to not care about something I really did care about. I can even pinpoint when this need for blankness began. In my last year of practising law, I was assigned a file on industrial forestry and came across the story of two moose found frozen to death in a clear-cut. "Those moose should have made it," the Cree man who'd found them said. "But the clearing was too big. They probably walked all night, but there wasn't any shelter for them to find."

That's it, I thought. I finished my report, and lasted a few more months at my firm, but that moment was the shutting-down point. I didn't like the way accounts of animal suffering made me feel. I'm no fan of stories about human suffering, but stories about animals hit me harder. In some ways, I'm still that post-divorce eight-year-old, clutching my copy of *Charlotte's Web* and wondering where everyone in the house went. It was essential to me that Wilbur, the pig under threat of death, be saved. His survival was a deftly coded message that kids facing tough times would make it through as well. If Wilbur had died, the pint-sized version of me would have lost a crucial bit of hope.

So my storyline for psychological reassurance goes like this: the pig makes it through; it's saved by love; and it goes on to return that love to everyone around it, creating an unending spiral of warmth and good feeling. I couldn't make stories about wolves being hunted by helicopter fit this story line. And the fact that such stories didn't fit always made me feel like something inside me was exploding – *Wilbur is dying* – and this felt so awful that all I could do was turn away.

But I was starting to realize that turning away was coming at a cost. My experience with local place was teaching me that belonging is always rooted through caring. If you don't care, you won't connect, because there's nothing to connect to. And if you limit your concerns to things you barely care about, you'll get a watered-down form of belonging, because your deepest feelings won't be in play.

As I reflected on this idea, I realized that I must have already understood some aspect of this when I had left the

cat care session at the Humane Society the previous
October and told myself I'd have to find a different way of
connecting with animals. Although I hadn't really fleshed
out the idea at the time, I'd meant a different *nice* way. I
had visions of fostering feral kittens and turning them into
their sweetest, most sociable selves. It was my vet, Dr. Ted,
who'd disabused me of this notion. I'd taken Hodge in for
a checkup the following May. He'd lost even more weight,
and he was starting to wobble when he walked. I noticed
how exposed Hodge looked on the examining table – the
harsh light showing every speck of dander on his black fur –
and as Dr. Ted was feeling for something under his ribs,
I said, "I'm thinking of fostering."

Dr. Ted didn't look up. "Fostering?"

"Kittens. You know, homeless ones."

Now Dr. Ted lifted his gaze from Hodge to me. "That's
a *terrible* idea," he said, clearly not feeling any need to sugar-
coat his response. "A feral kitten could be carrying anything. And Hodge can't handle vaccines. A sick kitten
would finish him off."

Dr. Ted was holding Hodge firmly between his hands.
He looked like he wasn't going to let go until I promised
not to foster.

"I won't," I said sheepishly. Dr. Ted lifted one hand.

"I *promise* I won't," I added. He then lifted his other
hand, returning his attention to Hodge after smiling at me
like I'd passed some test.

Hodge was a problem. If I wanted to keep him safe, I
couldn't foster cats or small dogs. Dr. Ted even warned me

about volunteering at animal shelters, since I might carry viruses home on my hands or clothes. Sitting with Hodge in my armchair, our orange throw draped behind us, I asked, "So what should I do, mister?"

I could feel his feet digging into my thighs. Sitting on anything but soft surfaces was now uncomfortable for him, and he seemed to be testing my legs to see if they counted as soft. I guess they did, because he settled into a crouch and looked at me. His eyes were wetter now that he was sick, and I felt my throat tighten at the mere thought of him feeling any distress.

But maybe that was what I needed to tune in to. I didn't blank out on what was happening to Hodge. In fact, caring for him in old age made me feel even more connected to him than I had when we were younger. If I could somehow recreate that sense of care in relation to other animals, I thought, I'd be confronting the blankness that had sprung up in me. I'd be cultivating deeper feelings in relation to something I cared about, and – if my experiences in the garden held true – this act of caring should lead to a fuller sense of connection.

But when I tried to think beyond homeless cats and dogs, I wasn't sure of what to do. I tried to apply the lesson I'd learned at the Humane Society orientation: if a goal seems right but the fit is wrong, then branch out. And I did branch out, but I kept running into the same problem: many stories of animal suffering were transmitted from faraway places, and there wasn't much I could do about the Congolese bushmeat trade from my apartment in Toronto.

Or, there was something I could do: I donated money to groups like the Jane Goodall Institute that were tackling the trade head-on.

"But I'm not sure that's enough," I said. I was on the phone with Laura. It was one of our usual hour-long conversations. I'm not sure how we'd gotten on to the subject of me donating money. Our talks were wide-ranging, but they didn't usually hit on monkeys. (Animal suffering wasn't Laura's "I can't take it" subject. Endless, illegal confinement was.)

"It's better than doing nothing," she replied. "You might be paying someone to care on your behalf, but at least you're doing something."

"But I want to do more. I feel I should do more."

"Why?"

"Well, I used to."

"And you made the decision to stop. For good reason." She knew my frozen moose story. "I'd respect anyone who says the world is so terrible now they have to turn away. You can't force anyone to care."

"But I'm so fascinated by the people who do care. I hear about these reports about torture from Human Rights Watch, and I think, 'Who *writes* these things?'"

It wasn't a rhetorical question. As a human rights lawyer, Laura had crossed paths with a lot of people who'd gone into the field to work in this area. We both knew a woman who'd spent a year documenting war crimes in Sierra Leone. For Laura, especially, a job recording human rights violations wasn't unthinkable. She just didn't want to do it.

"It's burnout work," she said. "People go to these places for a year, or a half-year. And they wind up vicariously traumatized. It's not sustainable."

"But they're totally engaged."

"Yes, and those people are the exceptions. You're thinking of this in terms of extremes. If you put donating money at one, and volunteering to go to a war zone at ten, most people are going to wind up somewhere in between."

"Where are you?"

She gave it some thought. "I'm probably a four. I read all my materials from Amnesty, but when the details get too awful, I stop. On a really strong day, I might be a five. But what Mita did?" This was our friend who'd gone to Sierra Leone. "That's not me. It's too much."

Laura was referring to fit, and I had to say she was right. No matter how qualified she might have been, it was hard to see her collecting stories of atrocities for months on end. But she was still several rungs above me on the caring ladder.

"I want to be a four, too."

"You're being competitive about caring?"

"It's motivating."

Something had to motivate me. It wasn't just that Laura was more connected than me, and that her ability to care was part of this. It was that there weren't many models of reasonable caring available. All the stories I came across tended to be what Laura described as "tens" – peace workers enduring captivity in the Middle East, or women devoting their lives to filming every factory farm in England.

It was clear that I needed something less intense than this. I'm probably grittier than Laura – the child of divorce, the demolished neighbourhood, and so on – but I wasn't so gritty that I could sleep on the ground under an anti-malaria net in South Sudan. I had to find a way of caring at home, at a level I could handle and in a way that felt meaningful to me.

This shouldn't have felt like a radical thing to aspire to, but in some ways it did. When Laura talked about vicarious trauma, she was referring to people who worked with torture victims. But there's a notion that exposing ourselves to *any* sort of suffering might lead to psychological damage. When I was trying to figure out why my caring project felt so counterintuitive, I came across a self-help column that advised shutting out bad news: "Negative influences will permeate and influence your consciousness. When following news creates anxiety or depression, it's time to turn it off."

What struck me as interesting about the clipping wasn't its advice ("Turn off the media! Turn off the media!") but rather the fact that I halfway believed in what it was saying. I wasn't sure where I had picked up the lesson, but I'd absorbed the idea that if I turned to what upset me, something *bad* might happen.

Experts who write about caring know that many of us think like this, and they see the thought itself as evidence of how disconnected we've become. If we didn't feel so alone, they argue, we wouldn't feel the need to protect ourselves so much. Caring, write experts like the theologian Henri Nouwen, almost always requires a group. In losing groups – and of the dozens of major, nationwide organizations that existed in 1900, very few are left – we've lost the vehicles that used to help us care. When I started this project, I thought that my reluctance to care had to do with abuses being worse today than they were a hundred years ago. In the case of developments like factory farming or boatloads of migrants lost at sea, they probably are worse. But the one-hundred-year comparison is a tough one to draw, since it hauls you smack up against the First World War, which can hardly be described as the high point of human kindness. When I thought about it further, I realized that what had changed wasn't barbarism, but rather the new expectation that we face it alone.

It was clear that the first thing I had to do was stop trying to face things alone. I had to find a group that would help me respond to the problems I cared about most. Trying to recreate what the older organizations used to offer, I decided I needed a group that was local, met regularly, and addressed animal issues. There weren't a huge number of groups that fit these criteria – a fact I'd come to understand more fully in my volunteering project – but I did remember Greenpeace. Despite its international reputation and media savvy, I knew that Greenpeace still had local offices, relied on volunteers, and addressed both global and regional environmental issues.

I went online and found a volunteer orientation session scheduled for mid-June. I arrived on a warm night, and I liked the office immediately. I think there's a bylaw somewhere saying that all environmental non-profits have to be decorated along the same lines: reclaimed hardwood floors, halogen lights, ferns, and posters featuring either old-growth trees or grizzlies. I breathed in the nicely oxygenated air and admired a row of birch trunks serving as a wall. The trunks were truncated – they stopped at the ceiling – but they created a lovely *trompe l'oeil* effect of lifting up through the roof, as if the branches were stretching straight into the sky.

I took my spot in one of the last empty chairs, which were arranged in a semicircle around the coordinator. Clara was a gleeful young woman with chipmunk cheeks, glossy black hair, and a Twitter-themed T-shirt that read #TARSANDS WTF??? She seemed pleased to see such a good turnout – the twenty chairs were nearly full – and I smiled as she gazed around the room, murmuring, "Rad."

Clara began by explaining that a lot of people misunderstood Greenpeace – it was more than whaling ships and people rappelling down buildings – and she said that to familiarize us with their major campaigns, she'd show us two videos. The first was about their anti-nuclear campaign, and I found it interesting. I hadn't seen footage of Chernobyl in over twenty years, and the film ended with the unintentionally mixed message that nuclear fallout might be a positive thing, since the exclusion zone around the reactor looked awfully green.

Then Clara introduced the next video, which was about tigers being killed in Indonesia. "This might be hard to watch," she said in a *buck up* tone of voice. "But it's short."

The funny thing was, I did buck up. It was the sort of video I couldn't have faced alone – the sort of thing I would have hit "stop" on instantly if I had been watching at home. But watching it in a group was different. The video was horrifying, with footage of tigers caught in big metal traps. The cats were circling and pacing; their forelegs were bloody and their eyes were full of terror. I cringed, but I could feel everyone around me cringing too. When I looked across the semicircle, I saw the woman opposite me wearing what I knew was my own expression: tense brows, squinted eyes, teeth tight along her lower lip. Watching the movie wasn't fun, but it seemed to be leading, if not to togetherness, then at least to a shared response that might form the basis for it.

In fact, as I would come to learn, and as Greenpeace quite likely already knew, shared distress is a freeway leading straight into belonging. We tend to think of belonging in positive terms – say, me trimming back squash vines with Heidi in the sun – and while good experiences do lead to belonging, they don't always get you there as fast as hard ones.

When North American airspace closed on 9/11, planes crossing the Atlantic had to stop somewhere. For a lot of these planes, the first available spot was Gander, Newfoundland. Gander had been a military training base for decades, so while the town was small, it had jet-sized landing strips and a big air traffic control tower. On September 11, forty-two jets carrying seven thousand passengers landed in a town of just eleven thousand people. This could have been a disaster – thousands of frightened passengers, no hotels, and locals unaccustomed to strangers. But something else happened. Residents from Gander and the surrounding towns immediately drove to the airport to take the strangers in. They opened up their houses, provided food, celebrated birthdays, and helped steady people whose lives had been thrown off course by events they could barely believe. Some of the friendships forged from those events have continued, with people from Germany and New Jersey still trekking to Gander to celebrate the ties they made at such a terrible time.

It's a key aspect of belongingness research: shared distress pulls people together. In fact, as I would come to learn, it can pull you together with others incredibly quickly and in a profound way. But you can only get to that fuller stage of togetherness by acting. Just sitting around and feeling bad doesn't accomplish much. It would be like all the Gander residents staying in their houses, watching scenes of the airport on TV and saying, "Oh, how terrible."

To connect, you have to act, and Greenpeace was offering ways to do so. The nuclear campaign didn't appeal to me – it had to do with approval hearings, which sounded dull – but I snapped to attention as Clara began to describe the tiger campaign.

"The tigers are being killed because loggers want the trees, but they can't cut the trees down because they're considered tiger habitat. So the loggers are solving the problem by getting rid of the tigers. That's pretty bad," she said, in something of an understatement, "but it's even worse that companies in our city are buying paper from these people."

She started to walk back and forth in front of our semicircle. "One of the biggest buyers is KFC. Customers don't know where their chicken buckets are coming from. So we need to tell them."

Now she stopped and looked at us. "What we need people to do is, well, two things. Some people will dress like tigers, and some will dress like Colonel Sanders, and we'll leaflet so that customers connect their chicken dinner to what's happening overseas."

It wasn't such a crazy idea. In fact, Greenpeace's international campaign targeting KFC and other major corporations ended up being so successful that the company destroying tiger habitat made a promise to stop. At the time of my meeting, though, this outcome was still a long way off, and I didn't like the way the thought of dressing up like Colonel Sanders was making me feel.

It wasn't just the prospect of the outfit (though I look terrible in white). It was that dressing up and standing on a street corner felt embarrassing. Even if I didn't dress up – and Clara seemed to understand that some people wouldn't want to – I'd be out leafleting for a cause. It seemed so marginal. Looking back, I wince at what I'm about to say, but it seemed so *uncool*. When I finally regrouped and got myself to a street corner, though it ended up being for a different cause, I was in fact told that what I was doing was uncool, though people didn't always use that word, sometimes preferring variations such as *lunatic*, *dimwit*, and *loser*. Although it took me some time to understand it, I finally realized that it wasn't my particular form of caring that was being judged; it was caring itself. There was something unhip about it, something others didn't like.

To learn that lesson, though, I had to find a different group. Even though I left Greenpeace thinking that I didn't want to demonstrate, I was still committed to caring. So I continued to read the news and google Meetup groups, trying to find an organization that would let me care without introducing the Colonel Sanders angle.

And then, in early July, I chanced on an article about a group called Pig Save. Toronto's nickname used to be "Hogtown," because of the number of pigs that met their end there. I was surprised to learn that one of these abattoirs was still operating, right downtown and in the middle of a bunch of new condo towers. The details of the transport horrified me. Pigs were trucked in from hours away. The ones who died en route were the lucky ones, since the rest were left to vomit on each other while stumbling around in feces and urine. Trying to draw attention to the pigs' plight, and to the problems of factory farming in general, was Pig Save. It held vigils near the abattoir, passing out information and trying to lend some comfort to the animals as they were driven to their deaths.

Pig Save. The group couldn't have picked a more compelling name. It was *pigs*. It was *Wilbur*. This was my chance to pay back a debt to a childhood friend, or to his injured sisters and brothers, and maybe – in a *Charlotte's Web*–inspired daydream – save one who'd be my friend forever.

The prospect of joining the vigil still made me uncomfortable, but at least now I had something to draw on to counter that discomfort. I visited the group's Facebook page and saw a vigil coming up that Sunday afternoon.

Checking off my connection criteria – the group was local, it met regularly, and it had members who seemed to see each other weekly – I made the decision to go.

That Sunday, I packed my belongingness bag and headed to the intersection named online. I was surprised by how big it was. There were three lanes of traffic running north and south, with streetcar tracks down the centre, meaning it was an eight-lane roadway transecting a four-lane roadway, with people on the sidewalks in every direction. Again, although I wasn't sure where it was coming from, embarrassment hit. I'd have preferred a baby-steps sort of process for my first demonstration. The prospect of starting to publicly care at one of the biggest intersections in town seemed overwhelming.

So I stayed on my side of the street and waited to see what would happen on the other side, where people were beginning to collect. A woman about my age was unfurling a pink banner that read SAVE THE PIGS. Two men with dark hair and pig masks upturned on their heads were helping her string it between a hydro pole and a flagstaff. Then another man arrived, who looked normal enough until he pulled on a long black cloak, grabbed a plastic scythe, and donned a gigantic plastic pig head.

My sense that caring was going to involve doing something strange just intensified. Should I cross the road and join them? They didn't just seem unusual – though I never had seen a porcine Grim Reaper – they also seemed so vulnerable. Five of them were standing right at the edge of the road, holding posters above their heads and opening themselves to whatever abuse or insults might be hurled at them. I'd heard a manic shout of, "I love BACON!" and I also heard a lot of car horns, though I didn't know what the honking meant.

Could I do it? Could I join these people and be as vulnerable as them? I saw their vulnerability as both a bad and a good thing. Bad, because it meant they were completely unprotected – there was nothing between them and the traffic except their flimsy plastic signs. Good, because none of these people could be vain or self-centred. If they were, they wouldn't be risking social suicide by standing beside the road and proclaiming their love of pigs.

Their humility finally won me over. With the question, *Why did the chicken cross the road?* repeating itself in my anxious brain, I personally crossed the road and made my way to the dark-haired woman who seemed to be the leader. She was pretty, with dark eyes and a natty all-white outfit: white sneakers, white shorts, white T-shirt. On the top of her head sat a little pink baseball cap.

"Beth?" I asked, holding my hand halfway out. Her name had been in the newspaper. I wasn't sure of what else to say. I tried to come up with something. "I saw the article in the *Star* and thought I might help."

She smiled, and I recognized her. We had worked for the same law firm years earlier. She'd been hired to collect signatures in support of an endangered species bill; I'd been hired to work on the bill. We'd even briefly shared an office, as I recalled. I didn't mention any of this, though. Even though I'd crossed the road, I was still leaving myself plenty of room for crossing back. Mentioning a previous connection would compromise this, so I remained silent.

Beth didn't seem to recognize me. She just greeted me warmly and waved toward a plastic tub of cookies sitting on a ledge. "Do you want one?" she asked. "Mitch brought them. They're almond. Vegan. Very tasty."

I shook my head no. I was too nervous to eat.

I think Beth noticed this, but she didn't mention it. She was keeping her voice low and even, as if to steady me. In fact, she sounded the way Terri or Chris might if they saw me having some sort of anxiety attack.

"Would you like to poster or pamphlet?" she asked in this soothing tone.

"Poster," I managed to spit out. I'd already noticed that pamphleting meant going right up to people and trying to hand them a fact sheet about the abattoir. If I postered, I wouldn't have to say anything. I partly recognized that refusing to talk to strangers was contrary to the whole notion of connecting, but I didn't care. There was only so much interaction I could handle at that point.

"You can stand with Rick and Marcia," Beth said, leading me to an older couple standing beside the road. "They know the drill."

It sounds simple enough – Beth deciding, after chatting with me, to introduce me to people who'd been there before – but this was an important gesture. Without giving me any sense that she was doing so, Beth was responding to my anxiety by pairing me up with people I could talk to and who could show me the ropes. Rick, helpfully, wasn't wearing pig ears or a cloak. He looked totally ordinary – the sort of guy who might have a day job managing an Olive Garden – and he was good at keeping up a stream of breezy chatter while holding a sign that said HONK FOR MERCY FOR PIGS.

"You've got to hold it up, honey," he said after I had stood frozen beside him for five minutes with my poster at my hips. My sign read WHY LOVE ONE BUT EAT THE OTHER? and had a photo of a puppy beside a piglet. I didn't want to lift it. I might have made it to the demonstration, but I was still in baby-steps mode. Being there was one thing. Lifting the sign was something else.

A car honked, and I thought it was an assault, or the prelude to someone charging out of their car to yell at us. Then I saw Rick give the driver a friendly thumbs-up, and I remembered that his sign said to honk in support.

"You mean people actually honk?" I asked. For some reason, the only reaction I had been expecting was hostile opposition.

"Lots of people," Rick replied. As if to underscore his point, two more drivers hit their horns. Rick smiled, and his wife – standing two feet down the road with her own pig poster – waved at them.

"Maybe not the people going to the highway," Rick continued. "They don't know. But lots of folks who live around here think it's awful."

"The abattoir?"

"Not just the abattoir. The trucks run sixteen hours a day. That's a lot of pigs to see if you're walking down the road or looking out your window."

"Will we see pigs today?" I asked. I felt slightly ashamed. In the midst of stressing about coolness, I'd kind of forgotten about the animals.

"Maybe, maybe not. The drivers try to avoid us here, because people will stand with us if they go past. So there's other routes they take."

"When do you see the pigs?"

"Morning vigils. Down by the lake. They have to take that road."

I was trying to sort this out – I hadn't realized there were two different sites – when Rick said, "Lift that sign. Here comes a bus."

The full extent of what was about to happen suddenly hit me. A packed lake-bound bus was stopping right in front of us. I could see people reaching for their cellphones and realized I was about to be posted to a hundred Flickr pages. This had the instant effect of making me do what Rick had been telling me to do – haul my sign up – but I had done it to cover my face and hair, not to broadcast its message. I could hear people laughing, and I thought I might actually evaporate with embarrassment when I heard a woman shout, "Way to go!"

My eyes were closed, but Rick said, "She means you."

Really? I'm nine-tenths ham; I had to see my admirer. I slowly lowered my sign and saw a woman with frizzy hair smiling as she gave me a big thumbs-up. Someone else was taking my photo, but I didn't care, because I was suddenly smiling at this stranger who cared about the same things I did. As the bus pulled away, she pressed her hand to the window and mouthed, "Go, girl." And it was so strange. The woman was gone, but I suddenly felt less alone.

It was that tease of connection that got me to the lakeside vigil. This was something of a challenge, since it started at seven and I'm not a cheerful early riser. But Rick had said that it was where the pigs would be, and since the pigs were what I wanted to see, I rolled out of bed at 5:45 a few days later and headed to the lake.

The location surprised me. When Rick had said that the vigil was at the lake, I had pictured us on grass near the water – a sort of gentle, private, bucolic space. In fact, I found Beth setting up on a traffic island smack in the middle of eight lanes of traffic. The road was so wide, and the traffic so heavy, that the island – which was only about ten feet across – served as a stopping point for people too slow or encumbered to make it through the lights in one go.

There was a visibility to the traffic island that alarmed me. I still hadn't gotten over my reluctance to demonstrate, and here there was no backdrop, nothing to blend into. It was like being in a spotlight. This didn't seem to bother the others. If anything, they seemed more motivated in this full-view setting than they had near the downtown towers.

"Why are we here?" I asked Beth. The park was just across the road, and we could have set up quite peacefully – and with way more camouflage – right under the trees.

"Because this puts us beside the turning lane," she explained, "and the trucks have to turn here. If they hit a red light, they have to sit. The drivers hate it, but it gives us a chance to get close to the pigs."

Right. The pigs. I realized that I had, in a way, gotten off easy at the first vigil. Not only had I been able to occasionally step away from the edge of the sidewalk and hide in the shade of an office building, but I hadn't actually seen any animals.

This morning was going to be different. There was an upbeat, expectant vibe to the proceedings. The Grim Reaper was joking about having tried to catch a ride to the lake, noting how hard it could be to get a lift when you were dressed like Death. Mitch was passing around more cookies, and another protestor was tucking his poster into a bull clip worn on a string around his neck so that he could keep his hands free for pamphleting. Everyone seemed relaxed, almost cheerful. Their high spirits reminded me of the fieldworkers I'd met while writing my endangered snake article, and I started wondering about the same sorts of things. What kept them going? Why were they willing to do this strange thing?

Then someone shouted, "Truck!" and I understood.

The light was green, and the truck was moving fast. I had to scramble to make sense of what was happening. The first thing I was aware of was a blanket-thick stench of urine and feces and filth. I was breathing this in while staring at the truck, which was silver, with slatted sides. Pigs were pressed against the slats, trying to get out, but all I could see were parts – a pink haunch through one slat, then a folded ear, a darkened snout. I was trying to fit the pieces together when I began to hear a high-pitched squealing sound. I thought it was the driver hitting his brakes, but this made no sense because the truck wasn't stopping. Then I realized it was the pigs. They were screaming. I heard a hard shuffle and fall as the truck took the corner, and I was left standing in a cloud of diesel and fear, the squeals fading as the truck disappeared.

The island fell silent. No one was moving or talking. Beth had brought her dog – a little beagle named Bean who she had left in the shade on the park side of the road – and I looked at him and in the next second burst into tears. I didn't know why I was crying. Everything just felt suddenly awful. The Grim Reaper patted my shoulder and said, "You'll be okay," but I needed to get off the island. As soon as the light changed, I crossed the street and walked straight to Bean. I told myself he needed comforting, but really, I needed him. I bent my head down next to his and pressed my face right into his fur. Then I breathed in the warm, healthy smell of him and I heard myself whisper, "I'm sorry."

That should have been the end of it. This wasn't caring in the manageable form I'd planned on. This was *bad*: the horrible smell, the chunks of flesh, the desperation. But it was still caring – in fact, it was a form of caring I'd never before let myself engage in. I had never exposed myself emotionally in that way, had never come so close to the suffering that I had said I couldn't take.

And a completely unexpected thing happened as I sat with Bean on the park side of the road. I realized I didn't want to *be* on the park side of the road. I wanted to be with the group, visible and protesting. My embarrassment – which just moments before had been palpable – was gone. What I had seen left no room for it. It was impossible for me to go back to the language of *cool* or *marginal* after hearing that braking sound, the sound of the screams.

So I crossed back to the traffic island, and when the next truck came by, I was steadier. This truck stopped for longer, and I could see more. The slats were about four inches high, and there were more bodies pressed up against them. I could study the soft pink fur around one pig's bleeding ear, or survey the scars down a haunch, or see an eye, just one frightened eye, above sagging bags filled with pus. I was seeing all of this, but in a sense I was looking at the scene through a shared point of view. Everyone on the island was seeing the same things and feeling the same intense emotions. And so long as those emotions remained raw, I personally didn't matter. All during that vigil – and at least six trucks went by that morning – there would be moments when my own consciousness would spring up again. I'd realize I was hot, or uncomfortable, or that I'd lowered my sign. But until that happened, I was with the others in the most astonishing way: the shared response was so strong we simply were no longer separate.

It's hard to overstate how powerful this mind-meld experience can be. Gregory Walton, a psychologist at Stanford University, has shown how simple feelings of connection – like realizing that you and a stranger share a birthday – can lead to a shared sense of allegiance. In trivial contexts, this might make you change your preferred brand of soft drink or like what your new friend has on her iPod. In non-trivial contexts, it can change who you are and what you believe in. Belonging can turn you, in some very important respects, into a different person.

That's what makes this form of belonging tricky. The intensity feels really good. But culturally, we're not used to it. Stepping out of individualism into a shared group response is like travelling from one country to another and suddenly realizing this new place you've arrived in is awfully satisfying – maybe even a place you don't want to leave. And if you don't want to leave, then you have to do whatever's necessary to keep your passport.

So a strange thing happened that morning at the vigil. I went from being embarrassed about caring to wanting to demonstrate my caring in the most overstated way. I have to stress that no one from Pig Save ever said that I needed to expose myself to more suffering or put myself on the line. But I wanted to. At some level, I understood that the sense of belonging I was feeling flowed from shared distress, so my reasoning went like this: if I increased my sense of distress, my sense of belonging would skyrocket.

Beth seemed to get this, and in retrospect I can see that she was trying to ratchet me down. A lot of the old-timers in the group talked about the abattoir, which I hadn't yet seen. (Protesting outside the abattoir didn't make sense, since it was on a side road with little traffic.) Once, when we were standing on what came to be known as Pig Island, I heard Beth tell Mitch that the windows were covered now.

"What do you mean?" I asked, interrupting.

"Well, there used to be windows out back, with nothing behind them but the train tracks. So if you went around at night, you could see the pigs being led to slaughter. Or, really, you could hear them. They'd be screaming and screaming. They knew exactly what was going to happen."

"Can we go there now?"

"No. They figured out I was filming, so they covered the windows with planks."

"But you can still hear the screams?" I sounded strangely eager, even to myself.

Beth paused. She was up on trespassing charges for filming at the abattoir, and she had a lot of experience with truck drivers and pig handlers. She was quick to point out that some of these men were kind – I once saw a truck driver give us a quick and guilty thumbs-up – but she'd also been sworn at and threatened in ways that went way beyond taunts of, "Ham sandwich!" She was willing to go to court, but she didn't expect anyone to wind up in the dock with her.

"I don't mind," I said, sensing her hesitation. "I'm willing to get arrested." And here's the thing: I really was. I, the former lawyer with the air of unshakeable innocence, was willing to stand in front of a judge on charges of criminal trespass. I liked playing out this little scene in my mind:

JUDGE: Ms. White. I understand you hold a law degree?

ME: That's right, Your Honour.

JUDGE: Do I need to explain to you the nature of trespassing?

ME: No, Your Honour.

JUDGE: Should I bother asking why you intentionally broke the law?

ME: For the pigs, Your Honour.

And in the daydream I'd be shouting, attracting the attention of everyone in court. "They're being brutalized, Your Honour." My shouting would increase and two armed guards would grab me as I raised my fist revolutionary-style: "For the pigs!"

I loved this daydream, loved how rooted and glued in it made me feel. I recognize that I might be an extreme case, but my experiences of changing – of becoming someone a bit *different* from my former self – and of losing my individual perspective are in line with the research. I don't think either of these two things is bad in itself. Both are much better than feeling numb and disconnected. But we have so little experience with this sort of intensity that it can take us by surprise, and maybe change us in ways we're not ready for.

I, for one, was determined to walk around the abattoir. A lanky protestor named Norm – the one who clipped his poster to a string around his neck – volunteered to take me.

"There's not much you can see," he said. He didn't mean this as a warning, the way Beth might. He was just stating a fact. "They own a big chunk of land, and it's all private past the sidewalk. You can't get in very far."

I didn't care. I was going to bear witness where the pigs met their deaths.

The setting wasn't what I expected. The abattoir – all grey, with docking bays for the trucks and a series of low boxy buildings that must have been where the pigs were killed – was at the centre of what had once been an industrial area. But the surrounding nineteenth-century warehouses had been broken up into flats, and they had all gone hipster chic. The fire escapes were covered with plants and flags; big bouquets sat in apartment windows. The buildings' ground floors featured bike shops, bakeries, and cafés.

"Wouldn't this be a weird place to live?" I asked. Norm and I were standing between two brick pillars that must have once held a gate. Now there was no need for one, because there were cameras trained on the sidewalk. If we took one step onto abattoir property, we'd be caught on film.

"Most of these people want the abattoir shut down," Norm replied. "They might not be political, but they know it's an awful place."

"The screams and stuff?"

Norm shrugged. I found that the people who'd seen the worst abuses kept their memories to themselves; they weren't about to turn suffering into gossip.

The sky was as grey as the buildings, and the site was silent. One thing I'd already learned was that terrified pigs make a lot of noise. The silence meant no pigs were there.

"I've never figured out the schedule," Norm said. "Sometimes there's just nothing going on at all."

We stood on the sidewalk for a while, until it became clear that there was nothing to see. Then we walked north, through a quiet and very green stretch of park. I asked Norm where he was from.

"Edmonton," he said with a laugh.

"Did you do the whole hockey thing?" Norm was pretty big, but it was hard to picture him, with his pig ears and pamphlets, as a red-blooded Canadian male.

"I did, actually. I wasn't too bad. I just wasn't competitive enough. I never really cared who won."

I was on the brink of asking, "Can you imagine what your teammates would say now?" But I realized it didn't matter. One of the nice things about Pig Save was that you didn't have to talk about pigs all the time. The fact that you did this strange thing together opened the door to conversations that felt truly easy. Instead of talking about activism, I asked Norm about his move, about whether he had had culture shock when he got to Toronto. We sat on a picnic table for a while, chatting as he drank ginger ale. He had to catch a streetcar, but he let one after another roll by without making a move. We were very relaxed around each other. Since we had the group to hold us together, we didn't have to say much one-on-one. Mostly, we just sat and watched the streetcars. In Toronto, they're bright red, and that morning they looked nice against the green grass and grey sky.

"People think Toronto's this big, cold place," Norm said suddenly. "But really, a lot of people here are pretty great."

I thought about the camaraderie of Pig Island. The pats, the in-jokes, the way we'd started to dress Beth's dog in a pink Pig Save T-shirt.

"They are," I agreed. "They're really nice."

Things went on like this for weeks. Pig Island started to feel like a great good place in a way my local swimming

pool never had, and also in a way that was a bit different
from the community garden. The garden was nearby and
low-key; Pig Island was far-off and intense. But I had the
same sort of easy conversations in each place, conversations that would get picked up from week to week – about
who'd gotten into nursing school, who'd found an apartment, who'd lost a job. We weren't *always* protesting on
Pig Island. Sometimes we'd be exchanging recipes, or
talking about some blockbuster movie that had just come
out. If no pig trucks came by, morning vigils could start to
feel a lot like the garden, only with protest signs and snacks.
But when the pig trucks *did* go by, everything changed: the
mind-meld experience would snap into place, and I'd lose
my sense of self as I looked at so much sadness.

I never got used to the sight of the pigs. In fact, some
occasions left me feeling worse than I had during my first
lakeside vigil. One morning in September, a truck sat for
what felt like a long time – it had just hit a red and so was
still for over ninety seconds – and in this time, Beth and
Mitch began to reach into the slats and pat the pigs closest
to them. I watched Beth slowly trace her fingers down a
pig's damp forehead. She was leaning forward and speaking
to it gently, looking it right in the eye, making sure the pig
knew she was there. When the truck began to pull away,
Beth and Mitch stepped back reluctantly. I was still on the
far side of the island – somehow, I hadn't found the courage to reach in – and when Mitch clapped the side of the
truck and said, "Sorry, guys," I found myself crying all over
again: about the pigs' horrid lives, about their impending

deaths, about what our cultural tolerance for cruelty said about what might happen to *me* at some point.

The problem was never the pigs. The problem was that right when I thought I was past the whole embarrassment thing, it started to creep back in. Beth's interests were starting to change. The vigils were attracting a lot of press, and Beth wanted to build on this momentum by reaching a broader audience. There was a Pig Save fundraiser held on Toronto's Centre Island, and when Beth asked me to draw pink pig heads in chalk on the ground near the ferry terminal, with arrows pointing the way to the boat, I did so reluctantly. A little girl came over and asked if she could have some pink chalk too, and I snapped my stick in half to give it to her. When she leaned down and started her own pink drawing, I thought, *Terrific, I'm back to first grade.* Shortly afterwards, there was a Pig Save booth booked at a vegetarian food fair, and I spent most of my time talking to a guy at the PETA booth who was dressed like a cow. Conversation wasn't a problem – I liked the guy in the cow suit – but his gear reminded me of the discomfort I had felt around the Colonel Sanders outfit, which reflected how I felt about costumes in general. I was the sort of kid who usually dressed as a hobo for Halloween, because it meant I could wear my own clothes, only in a more ragged fashion and with an expert makeup job applied by Terri.

I've never liked standing out. I don't see this as a strength, or as some admirable sign of humility. I see it as a weakness. It means that I pay too much attention to what others think of me, that I overvalue fitting in. Researchers who study belonging also study what's called "the desire for acceptance." When I started reading the Fear of Criticism Scale developed by the University of Pennsylvania's Aaron Beck and McMaster University's Peter Bieling, the material started to feel less like a quiz and more like an objective description of my life. Is it important to me to be approved of by others? Yes. Do I get uneasy when I can't tell if someone likes me? Yes. Do I look for signs of approval? Yes. Do I try to be nice, not hurt others' feelings, do things to please others, and apologize a lot? Yes, yes, and double yes.

No one in the social science world says that the desire for acceptance is a failing. Trying not to hurt other people's feelings is hardly a mark of pathology. The difficulty is that people who get a boost from belonging, and who seek it out, are often the same people who have a strong need for acceptance. There's a reason for this: both drives are about engaging with others in ways that maximize inclusion. When I was at the community garden, or in the dolphin pod, my need for acceptance probably helped me find belonging there – it meant that I was nice to people, that I listened hard to what they were saying and was alert to what they might need.

When the need to belong and the need to be accepted fit well together – which is most of the time – they spur each other on. But when they wind up in opposition, the person seeking belonging can feel torn in half. If belonging is being held out to you in ways that seem socially unacceptable, or just off-kilter, what do you do?

This conflict came to a head for me in October, on the night of an annual all-night arts event called Nuit Blanche.

The event is headlined by major international artists who create elaborate outdoor installations, like thirty-foot, flood-lit piles of chairs. But the event creates unofficial room for smaller groups and people – young art school grads setting up small exhibits of their own, or environmental organizations displaying water-saving tap attachments. When Beth said that she was planning a Nuit Blanche event, this was the sort of thing I pictured: maybe a booth with some fly-ers on it, and a petition for people to sign to get the abat-toir shut down.

That wasn't what Beth had in mind. I arrived at the down-town street corner she had designated to find a scene that filled me with alarm. A pig-friendly craftsman had made a plastic sow crate that was painted grey and looked exactly like the real thing. Someone had decorated the crate with Christmas lights, so that it glowed in the dark, and a pretty young woman was pulling on an elaborate pig suit, so that she could climb inside to show how little room there was. Norm had bought glow-in-the-dark rings and necklaces at the dollar store, and everyone around the crate was shining. Beth had gone one step further and was wearing the same midnight gardening cap Heidi had worn, only it seemed way brighter in this context because we weren't *at* a garden – we were at a major downtown intersection in the middle of an arts event that attracted a million people a year.

I was standing as close as I could to the building behind us. All the bravery I'd learned and felt on Pig Island was disappearing fast, because there weren't any pigs around. I thought back to my project on home and wondered if all the

stress I was feeling was just the product of my own perceptions, if I was *seeing* this scene as crazy when it was in fact
commonplace. Then I realized that my perceptions weren't
off at all. This was theatre, and it was meant to provoke. But
I don't like to provoke. I like to *get along* with others.

So when a big beefy guy came up and started shouting,
I hid behind Norm.

"Jesus ate lamb!" he bellowed. There was no explanation for why he chose lamb, or even Jesus. He just kept
repeating himself, his voice growing louder and louder:
"Jesus ate lamb!"

Then a woman from our side piped up. "The Bible *hates*
animals," she shouted. "It says to *despise* the fish of the sea."

This was turning into a crazy-sounding back-and-forth
about the role of animals in the Bible – "Noah saved cre-
ation!" "It's all about people!" – when Beth, in her usual
calm way, stepped forward and said, "Maybe we can stop
this now?"

To my amazement, the big guy turned on his heel and
walked away. But his leaving didn't mark the end of something; to me, it marked the beginning. A fact that Nuit
Blanche doesn't publicize, but which everyone knows, is
that the event is a good excuse for all-night drinking. Beth
was already addressing this, telling the group to be on the
lookout for drunks. She couldn't have picked a worse thing
to talk about. The prospect of booze was just fuel on the
fire. We already had a fully lit sow crate, glow-in-the-dark
jewellery, and a woman in a pig suit. Beth was excited
about all of this, encouraging us to draw more attention

to ourselves. *More attention?* If we got any more attention, I might expire.

I'm not proud of what I did next, but I did it. I went up to Beth and lied.

"I wanted to come show my support," I told her, "but I'm meeting friends to go to the show. I'm supposed to be meeting them now."

"You have to go?"

"I'd love to stay, but, well . . . they're expecting me." I looked at my wrist as if I were wearing a watch. I wasn't.

"Okay," Beth said. "Thanks for coming by. It's going to be a long night for us."

"I know." That's why I was leaving. I gave her a hug and headed into the crowd on the street. There were people everywhere, and the anonymity felt merciful. No one was asking me to dress up, or travel around with a sow crate, or do anything at all that might attract attention. I sat on a bench about three blocks away and looked back. I thought I might be able to see the group, but they were lost in the crowd. This felt like relief, and the relief told me all I needed to know about Pig Save and its new activities: if this was the way things were going, I wasn't a member anymore.

It took me some time to understand that this was okay. I spent weeks feeling badly about Nuit Blanche, and then more weeks feeling badly about not wanting to go to a protest at a hog auction. But these things weren't right for me. I'd pushed myself really hard, and I had managed to care with and for the pigs themselves. Pushing myself in this way had been important, because it had gotten me over my need for blankness and shown me I could connect in ways I hadn't expected. But pushing myself even further, into what amounted to political theatre, was a step I couldn't take. That wouldn't require changing one aspect of myself; it would require changing my whole self. And this was something I couldn't do.

Finally, after struggling with it for weeks, I decided that my need to care in a way that felt appropriate was all right. I'd already drawn a line against sleeping on the ground in South Sudan, and I hadn't beaten myself up over that. I decided that a second line – no theatre, no over-the-top displays – was fine too. If I wasn't going to push myself to go to a war zone, I also wasn't going to force myself to do something fundamentally at odds with my own personality.

What mattered was that this was a decision I made personally after exploring different ways of caring. It wasn't a cave-in to the embarrassment I'd initially felt. That had been about caring in general, about my feeling that there was something wrong about publicly stating my concern for the pigs. Because there is pressure on us today to not publicly care. Caring in private ways – buying free-range eggs, making donations, or shopping for recycled notebooks – is fine. But taking that caring to the next level and joining with others is judged. That judgment is communicated in the message that we shouldn't care ("Turn off the media! Turn off the media!") as well as in the criticism that's unleashed when you show that you do.

It took me a long time to figure out why so many people would drive past Pig Island only to shout, "I LOVE HAM!" They'd do this sometimes even when the pig trucks were nearby, when the screams were audible and the smell of feces so strong it felt solid enough to swallow.

I think what these people were really saying was that they weren't connected. They might have been proud of this or embarrassed by it, but either way, they were affirming individualism – the idea that we're mostly on our own, mostly responsible for ourselves, and connected in only limited ways. The message from Pig Island ran counter to this: we were saying that we were connected, that what happened to other creatures affected us. This statement was off-message in our going-solo world, and the shouts and criticisms were meant to get us back on track, to eliminate the claim that we're more connected than we think.

So *expect* to feel out of sync with those around you if you reach out for this form of connection. If you try to find a group to care with, you probably will feel some sense of judgment, and that's because the judgment is real. But the censure is part of what makes this form of connection so powerful. You're rejecting not just a certain form of cruelty or mistreatment but an entire idea. Even KFC eventually got the message: sourcing decisions made in Kentucky could affect animals overseas. We're linked, even if the ties are sometimes hard to see. Respecting these links is harder than blanking out, but it takes you further, takes you some ways closer to hope. On Pig Island, I could imagine a different sort of world, one where the links between us are affirmed and applauded. Not *Charlotte's Web*, exactly, but something like it. A world where ties aren't denied, where it's okay to cry openly about the fate of a pig. Because you're connected to it, because it's not a stranger, and because – in an ideal world – neither of you are alone.

CHAPTER FIVE

Faith

What to Do If the Group You Want to
Belong to Doesn't Want You

IF CARING FELT SOMEWHAT counterintuitive, church
didn't. As soon as I started this challenge on belonging, I
knew I wanted faith to be a part of it. It almost had to be.
Attending church, mosque, or synagogue is one of the few
things people are still doing when it comes to belonging;
it's a piece that hasn't dropped out of the connection puzzle. And research shows that this sort of belonging works.
People who attend services routinely test as more connected than those who don't. It's sometimes not clear
whether the connection flows from belief in a deity or from
the simple act of showing up and seeing the same people
every week, but the results are consistent: if you want a
sense of belonging, a good spot to find it is in your local
place of worship.

That's not to say that this form of belonging isn't complicated. Even leaving aside the question of whether you
can or do believe, there are all sorts of issues about where
to belong and about whether the group you want to belong
to will have you. One thing I've learned in this challenge is

that many groups screen; even the dog-walking program at the Humane Society was really aimed at people confident enough to handle large dogs. Faith communities take screening to the next level. They often have explicit rules about who can or can't belong. Although this practice is exclusionary for some, it has a flip side: if you define the rules of membership, you automatically increase the sense of belonging for those who fit in.

I wasn't totally prepared for these hard and fast rules of inclusion and exclusion – which is a bit odd, since I was familiar with rules. Part of the reason I believed the research on connection and faith was that I had attended faith-based schools until I was sixteen and found an extraordinary amount of belonging there. This isn't the same thing as finding an extraordinary amount of faith. I wasn't a particularly religious kid. I was mildly obsessed with Mother Teresa, but I had no burning desire to be a nun. In fact, there were so many nuns and priests floating around in my childhood that I have no memory of them as individuals: they're just a clutch of grown-ups in long, cloakish outfits who stayed mostly out of the way as my friends and I got on with the business of connecting.

I know there are many people who have had terrible experiences in religious schools, but I'm not one of them. For me, Catholic school offered everything that I've come to learn is essential to belonging: shared values, shared activities, and a sense of matching that in this case was literal, since we all dressed the same. And there was a physicality to Catholic school that I absolutely loved. Girls might be more self-conscious now, but when I was a teen, there was an awful lot of lounging around on the lawn, lying with our heads on each other's stomachs or arms as we talked about boys, or dancing in the convent's studio, all of us clad in blue rompers as we did the jitterbug and the Charleston and just about every other dance that dated to when the convent was built. And there was the ease that came with long stretches of nothing: just hours of mass where the main event might be poking your kilt pin into the next girl's leg, so that she'd yelp and draw a reprimand which would soon be forgotten in the timeless atmosphere of church.

I lost all of this when I transferred to public school in grade eleven. I've since lived in other extreme environments – post-communist Prague, the Arctic Circle – but I have never again experienced that sort of culture shock. My house was beside a factory, but the new school I travelled to was three subway stops south, in the wealthiest neighbourhood in Canada. Kids actually said things like, "I wonder how many cars he'll total before his mom stops buying them for him?" (In the case of the heir to one paper fortune, the answer was three.) And with all the money came a sort of worldliness I'd never been exposed to. When I was seventeen, a friend said that he was spending Christmas at an ashram. Jesse was Jewish, and I politely asked if *ashram* was a Hebrew word.

He laughed outright. "It's not Hebrew, you idiot. It's Indian. You know? Like yoga?"

I nodded, but I didn't know. I spent my last two years of high school feeling constantly clued out. I was popular – cute, penny-loafered, and bobbed like Molly Ringwald – but secretly, I felt cut off from everyone. It was my first major belongingness lesson: belonging can look like it's in place to everyone around you even when you don't feel any belonging at all. The disconnect I was dealing with left me with a longing for the school I'd left behind, and at some point in my teens, the notion of belonging and the notion of faith just fused: I'd lost one because I'd lost the other, and a recovery effort would require them to appear hand in hand.

Not that I openly acted on this principle. By the time I hit university, and had traded in the whole *Pretty in Pink* thing for Coke-bottle glasses and men's fedoras, I'd stopped talking about religion. Most of my friends were atheist or agnostic, and although it took me some time to figure out the difference – atheism means you don't believe; agnosticism means you're willing to be convinced – I usually described myself in one of these ways as well. Or at least, that's what I did in public.

Privately, my spiritual life was more complicated. I was a bit like the vocal non-smoker who always winds up drunk at parties with a cigarette in hand. When things got rough – and by this I mean when I felt too alone – I'd find myself back in church. Never as part of a congregation, but as someone in need of one or two sessions of shared prayers and outstretched hands. Even an empty church was enough to do the trick. The familiar smells – floor wax, candle wax, flowers, and incense – prompted memories of my connected girlhood, and these memories were usually enough to trigger feelings of togetherness in the here and now.

Although I didn't know it at the time, I was acting on a strategy belongingness researchers explicitly suggest: if you need an instant shot of belonging, try to remember a time when you felt fully plugged in.

When I read about this tip, at the outset of my faith project, I decided to test it. I was a bit worried that the genie was out of the bottle – that awareness of the link between memory and belonging might kill the sense of belonging itself. To my surprise, it didn't. Armed with my ever-ready belongingness bag of notebook, pen, and water, I headed to the Catholic chapel at the University of Toronto on a warm day in April. This was right around the time that I was doing my water-walking laps in the community pool, and just before I joined the garden. This meant that my faith project was overlapping with a few other activities, but this felt natural to me: looking for connection in one area made me curious about finding it in others.

That day was bright, but the windowless foyer of the chapel was dark, so I had to spend a few moments squinting in the dimness before I got my bearings and opened the door. Then the light that hit was beautiful. The church was small but the windows were tall, and they were filled that afternoon with streams of sunshine that reached into the pews in stretches of pink and gold. More light was coming from the white candles near the altar, and the altar itself was surrounded with lilies and daffodils that had been set out after Easter. The heady scent of the lilies was cut with a hint of polish that must have been recently applied, since the pews were gleaming. The gloss made the seats look

welcoming, and as soon as I was in one, I forgot I was there
for experimental purposes. I later noted a "recollected feel
of community," but that hardly captures how good I felt:
how I felt suddenly safe and no longer alone. When I
closed my eyes, a sort of presence began to emerge. Not
God, exactly, but an almost physical awareness of everyone
who had sat in that pew before me, all of whom seemed to
be right there with me then.

By this point, I was beginning to recognize the genius of
groups, and for the first time in years, I thought about joining a congregation. There was a poster board near the
door, and as soon I'd had my fill of airborne togetherness,
I went over to read about an upcoming potluck, a science
and faith reflection group, a disarmament group. Knowing
there'd be more in the monthly bulletin, I grabbed one and
began to flip through. There was an ad for a trip to Galilee;
updates to the Sunday parking rules; and then a small
notice for a group called Courage.

The sense of belonging I had been feeling started to
waver. I wasn't, as my high school friend had suggested, an
idiot. I knew the Vatican had never been totally down with
homosexuality. But there was so much about Catholicism
that everyone just ignored; a big part of the religion seemed
to involve pledging allegiance to rules you knew you'd
never obey. The Church's stance against homosexuality
had always struck me as falling into this category: a sort of
knee-jerk prohibition that didn't prohibit much at all.

I was wrong. When Pope Benedict took the helm in 2005,
the Church started putting its money where its mouth was

when it came to its teachings against "homosexual acts."
Even the small chapel I was standing in was offering a
Courage support group to help gay congregation members
deny their same-sex attraction. Which meant that if you
were acting on such attraction – or, in my case, if you clung
to the hope of someday acting on it once again – you were so
far beyond the religious pale that you might as well not
bother showing up, because you didn't belong at all.

I dropped back into a pew, trying to absorb this pulse of
rejection. This was a lot more complicated than being shut
out of a yoga studio. I'm not sure anyone has ever tested
the effects of Tylenol on the social pain that comes with
being told that even heaven doesn't want you. The sense of
belonging I'd been toting around for years crashed so hard
I could almost hear it shatter on the ground. I should have
stood up and left with my head held high, possibly tearing
up bulletins as I went. But I couldn't. The group I'd always
thought I was part of was kicking me out, and I really didn't
know what to do. I looked around and noticed the light
still streaming in: a patch of pale blue was falling just to my
right. I tried to read or understand some message in it, but
I couldn't anymore. Nothing seemed aimed at me any longer. The candles looked cold; the flowers seemed far away.
I suddenly did stand up, because I realized that, far from
belonging, I was quite on my own – and in fact had been
for some time.

It took me a couple of weeks to recover, but I eventually
told myself that being evicted from my religion was a good

thing, since it turned me into any other ordinary person starting from scratch. As a sudden non-Catholic, I could try to join other religions and see what was involved in trying to find a sense of togetherness.

Looking around for another faith isn't too unusual. Many North Americans actively change faith groups, with most trading in the religion of their childhood for one that feels like a better fit. The practice has become so common there's even a name for it: "church shopping." And, like all types of modern-day shopping, there are websites available to help speed the process along.

I logged on to Belief-O-Matic, an online quiz run by the spirituality website Beliefnet, in late June, largely because it promised to answer the question of where I might belong. The site was tongue-in-cheek – it assumed no legal liability for my soul – but the quiz was semi-serious: did I believe in God? Did I expect my prayers to be answered? And what about the natural world – did a higher power create it, or was I more of a big bang kind of girl? It felt slightly strange to punch my beliefs into an online portal, but it felt even stranger to be told I'd make a great . . . Unitarian Universalist.

For the first time, I got a sense of how confusing belonging through faith might be, since I had no idea what a Unitarian Universalist was. I clicked on Beliefnet's short description – just as I was expecting, they were equality-affirming environmentalists – but I couldn't remember ever seeing a church sign saying UNITARIAN UNIVERSALIST. Baffled, I ran the name through Wikipedia, which provided a surprisingly detailed history of Unitarianism from the 1700s to today but gave me very little sense of who these people actually were.

So I traded my laptop for my cellphone and called Laura, who'd grown up in the United Church.

"Are Unitarians the same thing as United?" I asked.

"No," she answered. She sounded like she was in the middle of doing something else, like trying to decide which food colouring to use for icing. I could hear a spoon hit the side of a bowl as she said, "They're different. You don't have to believe in Jesus. They're more liberal. Maybe hippies. Or maybe that was just the Unitarian guy I used to know. He talked a lot about nudity."

I paused.

"Why are you even asking this?" she asked, as if she'd just heard the question.

"I took an online quiz, and it told me that's what I should be."

"A quiz?"

I filled her in on Belief-O-Matic: "You know, like was the earth created in seven days, or are the 'days' really long periods of natural time?"

She paused for a few moments before asking, "How comprehensive could a quiz like that possibly be?"

"It doesn't have to be comprehensive. It's just a starting point. We both have religious backgrounds, but a lot of people don't. They need a starting point."

"And what's wrong with a library?"

"Have you heard of the twenty-first century?"

"So we've created a database for religion?" she asked, laughing. Oversimplification annoys Laura, and she started asking the questions I was trying to ignore. "What kind of research have they done? And is every religion on their list?"

"That's not the point. The point is, you find somewhere to start."

"But you don't know what your starting point means. A good book on world religions—"

I cut her off.

"Look, the United Church is kind of similar, right? Like, I can be gay, and it's pretty green?"

"Yes, but I'm not sure that's how you choose a church. Just because you have the same lifestyle as someone doesn't mean you're going to share the same faith."

This was actually a fairly major point, but I chose to not to hear it. It was out of character for me to ignore Laura, but with the Catholic Church telling me that my lifestyle was a non-starter, it was all I was focusing on.

"I'm going."

"Then I wish you godspeed."

One of the reasons I wanted to attend a United Church was that there was one in my neighbourhood, and I thought it might serve double duty: it would let me belong through faith while also firming up my connection to place. I visited the church's website that night and was slightly dismayed to find it covered with photos of couples and groups. I realized that the church was advertising the connection people were seeking, but pictures of people who were already together made me wonder if there was any room for me to fit in.

Appearing at church made this mild sense of exclusion more acute. There was a hold-up near the doors, and I didn't understand what was taking so long. Then I realized that everyone who entered was flipping through a shelving unit for their *name tags*. The sight of the name tags left me feeling sort of stunned: this was way more sociability than I was used to at a service.

"Are you new?" a greeter asked. She wore a light cardigan over a sundress and was standing right beside the shelf. She looked practised in welcoming newcomers. "We can make you up a tag right now."

I didn't really want a tag. "I'm not sure I need one," I said evasively. "This is my first time here."

The woman smiled and didn't press the issue. In retrospect, I can see that she handled the situation expertly. Part of the reason people are still turning to faith for a sense of connection is that faith groups – especially ones that have been around for a long time – understand how hard it can be to just walk in the door. Many congregations have active strategies for dealing with newcomers. This woman had clearly been instructed to offer the tag only once: anything else would have felt like pressure. As it was, she just said, "Welcome," and left me to make my way in alone.

"Downstairs," she added when she saw me heading for the main chapel.

It turned out that in early summer, with so many parishioners already on vacation, services were being held in the basement. This wasn't as dreary as it sounds: the ceiling was high and the windows dipped low; one whole wall was painted a bright shade of purple. The problem was the space itself. I'd been picturing a big church where I could sit unnoticed at the back. Here, no matter which direction I went in, I walked straight into someone else. This should have been a good thing – it was the sociability I was looking for – but it felt very different from walking into the garden, or even a Pig Save gathering. Those groups were elastic, with people coming and going all the time. Here, everyone was acting like they'd known each other for years. It felt less like church and more like a wedding. There were back-and-forths about kids and grandkids, about who was going to the cottage and who'd spend the holidays canoeing.

This familiarity – which must have felt so good to others – made my outsider status feel electric. In fact, it must have been obvious, because one well-mannered, well-dressed man came over and said, "We can't leave *you* out, can we?"

I felt thankful as he took my hand and winked, but then alarm set in because his good deed was attracting the attention of others, who seemed to realize they should welcome me too. A small procession was forming – a whole line of potential well-wishers – and this had a distinctly religious effect, because I started fervently praying for them to stop.

And lo, my prayers were answered. A piano started up, haltingly at first, and then more lushly, and people began to take their seats. I sank into a chair and told myself that all I had to do was survive the next fifty minutes. This wasn't entirely true, of course. There were plenty of things I had to do in those fifty minutes, like standing for prayers and singing, but I responded to these demands by getting up slowly and, for reasons I didn't fully understand, only mouthing the words. It was more like fake participation than real involvement. When the service finally ended, the woman beside me smiled and asked, with exactly the right mix of curiosity and detachment, whether I was new to the area.

Others were sitting down, chatting with their neighbours, but I stood up.

"Yes," I answered, even though this was an outright lie. I'd been in the neighbourhood for over a year.

"Did you move here from somewhere else?" the woman asked. She was slim, and still seated, and she was arching her head up toward me as if our conversation were taking place in a bus depot and my route had just been called.

And just as I would have in a Greyhound station, I threw my bag over my shoulder, trying to tie off the ends of the talk as quickly as I could.

"Newfoundland," I said in a rush.

Right as she was opening her mouth to say something else, I left. It was astonishingly rude, but I simply did not wait for her next question. I could see light from the main doors bouncing down the basement stairs, and I made my way for it. I could feel half the congregation watching me, but I didn't care; if I made it to that bright light, I'd be saved.

And I was. I hit the doors, then the lawn, and a near-run got me back to my apartment in under twenty minutes. I sank into my armchair, letting relief wash over me, but the relief was short-lived because the look on the woman's face – her friendliness giving way to surprise – made me feel kind of bad. Had I done the wrong thing?

Flush with a mix of shame and confusion, I called Ron for his usual compassion and understanding. He was the perfect person for church-related bewilderment, since he was so religious. It wasn't just that he read everything from German theology to *The Purpose Driven Life*. He also listened to Christian rock, watched YouTube sermons, and had Pray as You Go downloads for long subway rides.

"Was I wrong for not sticking around?" I asked, feeling anxious. I described my jailbreak behaviour at church. "I mean, I did sit through the service."

"Well," he said pensively, "talking to your neighbour sort of is part of the service. Church is about community, so being involved in people's lives to strengthen and encourage them is a reason why you're there."

This wasn't the guilt relief I was looking for.

"*You* don't go," I said, challenging him. Despite his deep faith, Ron had been describing himself as "temporarily unchurched" since 1995.

"You have belief without belonging," I added. The phrase was from the late Berkeley sociologist Robert Bellah, but I didn't mention this.

"Belief without belonging," Ron repeated, pondering it. "I guess that is what I have. There's probably something wrong with that. I listen to sermons, but church provides a special place to practise what the sermon is all about. That might be love or patience or forgiveness, but you have to be in real relationships to really feel those things. And a congregation provides that."

"So was it wrong for me to leave?"

He laughed. "You're taking this way too hard. Maybe it was just the wrong fit."

"I was thinking about the Quakers," I said. "They were next on my list."

"What list?"

"Never mind." I couldn't imagine explaining Belief-O-Matic to a man who could quote Dietrich Bonhoeffer. "It's just something I read somewhere."

"Well, you won't have to say much."

This was true. In contrast to my unfamiliarity with the Unitarians, I knew a few things about the Quakers. A name came to mind – George Fox? – and although I couldn't pin him to a state or a year, I knew he was a religious dissenter and that his followers practised mostly in silence. I also knew that the Quakers had an awesome social justice record, doing everything from hiding escaped slaves before the Civil War to demanding the reform of prisons and asylums.

Walking into a Quaker meeting a few weeks later, I thought I'd found the perfect fit. The Quakers own a mansion near the University of Toronto, and in the meeting room a whole wall had been replaced with a huge pane of glass. Wooden chairs were set up in a semicircle, and each seat had a view of the garden out back, with its roses on climbers and – briefly – a slim black cat who sat on the fence and stared in at us like a curious goddess.

There weren't many people there when I arrived, which surprised me since it was eleven o'clock and the service was about to start. But this particular group of Quakers had a fluid sense of time, and people kept filtering in over the next twenty minutes. This should have been irritating, but it wasn't, because everyone just murmured a quiet hello and settled into their seats.

When I had told Laura I was going to try a Quaker service, she'd said, "That much silence would flip me out," but I didn't mind. It was like meditation with a vaguely religious undertone. I let my gaze soften until all I could see was an outline of light. It was jarring when someone stood and spoke, but I found you didn't have to look at the speaker, and most people didn't grandstand. Toward the end of the service, one woman rose and in a high, clear voice, sang, "This little light of mine, I'm gonna let it shine," and the rest of the congregation met her on the refrain, with the whole sunny room suddenly singing, "Let it shine, let it shine, let it shine."

Lovely, I thought, as a gradual shuffle and murmur began to ripple through the crowd. The service was over. An older, grey-haired woman walked to the front of the room to make a few announcements. There would be a lecture that afternoon about the crime of ecocide; another group would be meeting about a living wage; and of course there'd be coffee and bagels right after the service.

As soon as people began to move, a woman about my age settled comfortably into the chair behind me. I knew what she was doing; Laura had already told me that churches assign greeting duties to select members, and one of the things this woman was supposed to do was invite me to the social.

"Would you be interested in joining me for coffee?" she asked. Her tone was perfect: welcoming but without a hint of pressure. This was not a religious hard sell.

Even though I'd been expecting the question, I was surprised at how tense it left me feeling. There were easily fifty people milling around, and I assumed most of them would be showing up for coffee. I'm usually okay with unstructured social situations, but this felt different. Partly because it was charged – just as Ron had said, it was a way to practise the patience and love I was supposed to have been contemplating – but mostly because I felt an emotional, almost childish grinding in of my heels: I didn't want to go.

"Sorry," I said. "I've got an appointment." This sounded false even to me. It was noon on a Sunday. Where could I be going?

"Do you have any questions about the service?" she asked, in the same open tone.

"No," I said, lying again. I was confused by the fact that there didn't seem to be any rules guiding the service. But saying this would open the door to a conversation about Quaker beliefs, and that would seriously slow down my departure. Because no matter how calm I'd felt during the period of silence, this conversation was making me feel just like I had at the United Church: I wanted to get out.

To her credit, the greeter seemed to recognize how jumpy I was getting. She slid out of her chair and was about to leave when she remembered her duty. She gave me one more chance: "Would you be interested in going to the lecture this afternoon?"

It took me a second to remember the subject: the crime of ecocide, or killing nature. Right up my alley, but I said, with a hint of regret, "Sorry. My appointment."

She nodded and gave me a slightly quizzical smile. It's not good form to lie in church, and the greeter seemed to know I wasn't telling the truth. But the prospect of joining struck me as – well, as something I didn't want to do. Leaving seemed far more attractive than getting to know others in the group.

As I headed out, winding my way past the mansion's big windows, I beat myself up for my introversion. An extrovert, I told myself, would have gotten her ass to that coffee klatch without so much fuss and evasion.

I'm not sure now that introversion was the problem. I think that without even noticing it, I'd started tumbling around in a rejection spin cycle. When I had read the anti-gay notice in the Catholic bulletin, I had understood that I was being rejected in a way that went beyond ordinary social pain. This rejection was *big*: codified, advertised, preached from pulpits. It was rejection from an entire institution purporting to speak on behalf of God.

This had overwhelmed my high pain threshold. I was left with no real way to respond, other than to express my anger. Belongingness experts study rejection closely, and the general consensus is that those who are rejected will still want to belong, and will often try to belong, but will do so while feeling pretty pissed off. With no way to direct their anger, they wind up engaging in pro- and anti-social behaviour at the same time. In short, they end up like me: openly looking for a new church but then behaving like children as soon as they step in, lying to the people around them, or refusing to talk, or just bolting as soon as someone makes eye contact. It was like I was running a rejection scorecard: the Catholic Church had rejected me, but I was rejecting the Quakers and the United Church. Which put me, according to some weird calculus, ahead in the game.

Or sort of ahead. Or not ahead at all. Because by August, more than three months after seeing the Courage ad, I still didn't have a congregation. By this point, someone might reasonably ask why I was still bothering. Throwing in the towel and walking away is a very legitimate response to what's known as the "porcupine problem" (meaning you head into a group looking glossy, but your quills go up as soon as someone tries to approach).

In some contexts, withdrawal makes sense. I've left book groups without a second thought. But withdrawal is only an option if the domain in question doesn't matter much. For some people, religion might fall into this "optional" category. For me, religion felt woven in. I'd had some form of faith in place for my entire life. In fact, the faith predated me, since my family had been Catholic for generations. And my ancestors had faced a more radical rejection problem and solved it in a more radical way. When they were told, in England in the early 1700s, that they could basically no longer be Catholic, they boarded boats for the New World and left the motherland behind. At some unconscious level, I was aware of my ancestors' tenacity. They'd crossed the ocean in rickety ships to protect their beliefs. Was I seriously going to give up because of an ad in a pamphlet?

I felt some encouragement being handed down the generations – *Stick with it, sister* – but I wasn't sure that Catholicism itself was what I had to stick with. My ancestors were some pretty hardline people. The intensity of their belief made them almost evangelical in their faith, and this made me wonder if what I should be searching for was a sort of evangelicalism. Maybe Laura was right: maybe your attitude toward the environment didn't determine your faith as much as your appetite for zealotry did.

So I regrouped. Toronto is not a very evangelical city; the big mega-churches are in the suburbs, and it would be hard for me to get to them, especially on a regular basis. I needed an urban evangelicalism, and I remembered the billboard that used to sit near my house before I left for Newfoundland. It was for the Alpha course. I recalled some promise about it enriching my relationship with God. When I logged on to the website, I immediately encountered the language I was expecting: "You are weary. Where is this all headed? Is there more to life than this?" After a lot of metaphors – boxes opening, lids lifting – I was assured that Alpha would open the door to deeper belief. All I had to do was try.

I was willing to try. Not only did the website hint at the intensity I was seeking, but it was structured in a deceptively smart way. Everyone who attended would be new. Alpha clearly recognized how hard it could be to join a congregation, and they had solved the problem by replacing an established congregation with a group of first-timers.

The first meeting was in September. The introductory dinner was held in the basement of a downtown church.

The ceilings were low, and the lights were too bright, but there was a pleasant enough atmosphere as we were served a simple meal of fish and bread. There were actually two Alpha courses that night – one for beginners, one on Christian parenting – and the twenty of us sat comfortably at card tables, talking about topics that weren't charged at all: the unfairness of the tax code, someone's problem with her hip. The crowd was mixed. It was the women serving us who were surprisingly high-end; the coordinator had a gym-slimmed body, sleek hair, and tall leather boots that might as well have been stamped with dollar signs. I'm not sure why I thought evangelicals would be dowdy. Maybe I was thinking of my forebears, with their no doubt wild hair and ragtag clothes. The evident wealth of the leaders disappointed me: it was hard to imagine rich people speaking in tongues.

Still, I was ready for charisma, and some of it was on display when we were moved to a sitting room full of mismatched armchairs and shown our first video. I hadn't really understood that most of the course would involve watching videos, but the star – Alpha's founder, Nicky Gumbel – oozed charisma. He started with the big-ticket item I was expecting: a lot of us were feeling empty, and God was the answer to that emptiness. I wasn't sure that this was true, but it wasn't what I was interested in. I was trying to figure out whether a group formed around the beliefs Gumbel was pushing could help answer that emptiness.

The video left me feeling energized; it was expertly shot, with Gumbel looking and sounding smart in a fancy British church. The content could have been taken from a grade ten religion class, but that didn't matter, because Gumbel's enthusiasm was contagious. He was so certain about what he was saying – about Jesus filling us up and giving us the energy we need to reach out to others.

I expected that this was a point we would debate. When the video ended, I was waiting for a rich exchange, for the sort of connection that comes with hammering out ideas with people who care passionately about the same things as you.

But that didn't happen. Tabbi, our group leader, was young, nervous, and wearing a snagged silk blouse that didn't match the glamour levels of the other leaders. Her voice almost shook as she began the discussion.

"What would you say to Jesus if you saw him today and could ask him one question?"

Silence hit. I couldn't fix the setting. Where would this conversation be taking place? Starbucks? A grocery store? I was still struggling with this – would Jesus appear all illuminated at my local doughnut shop? – when I heard a young woman say, "Suffering? Maybe I'd ask him about suffering?"

I peered beyond the wing of my chair to see the woman leaning forward. She had her hand slightly raised, like a student trying to answer a difficult question in class.

"Excellent," Tabbi said, looking relieved that someone had answered. "Why does God allow suffering?"

Why does God allow *suffering*? I could feel my brain trying to escape through my ears. I knew the leader was trying to initiate some sort of sharing, but it was like asking people to board a train that was rocketing past. There was just no way of getting a handle on this.

I tried to flag the problem. "I think the Church has been trying to answer that one for a long time," I said. "A really long time," I added.

Tabbi flashed a desperate look my way. My answer wasn't the personal one she wanted.

I paused. I could have rescued her. There was probably a way of reframing the question so that others could respond. As it was, everyone was fidgeting, looking either embarrassed or mildly alarmed. It was like being at an extremely awkward dinner party with no booze to cut the strain.

Things unfolded like this week after week. There was an emotional short-circuit no one could fix. We'd get the high-energy, expertly produced Nicky Gumbel video, then someone would turn off the TV and the room would fall dark. We'd be given snacks. Then the questions would start – either unanswerable ("Was Hitler born good?") or just completely beside the point ("What item would you bring with you to a desert island?"). The sharing people were there for never materialized. I eventually realized that our increasingly stressed and dishevelled leader was taking the questions from a guidebook, and I wondered what its authors envisioned: a debate about the nature of evil? I was trying to figure out what was going wrong when, at the start of week six, Tabbi, now bundled in layers of sweaters like she was trying to physically hide, said, "Everything in this session is optional. You don't have to participate if you don't want to."

Bingo. That was what had been missing. Choice. It wasn't just that Tabbi couldn't match Gumbel in terms of charisma; it was that you can't build group feeling by force. Suddenly, the energy level in the room shot up, catching Tabbi by surprise. Her thinking was almost audible: *You mean this was all I had to do all along?*

Everyone decided to participate. That week's subject was prayer, and after watching the video – Gumbel had a strange approach to prayer, in which he kept a ledger of which prayers were and weren't answered – we were all given the chance to offer up one thing we'd like the group to pray for. People pulled their chairs in closer. The room, which was drafty, started to feel a bit warmer. People talked briefly but very directly about money problems, problems with housing, concerns about a daughter. When it came to me, I said, with the first real honesty I'd ever expressed in the course, "My cat is sick, and I love him dearly." Hodge, who already had kidney disease, had just been diagnosed with cancer. Dr. Ted had said there was nothing to do but to be gentle and wait for nature to take its course. When I was away from home, I tried not to think of Hodge, because the thought of his worn-out self waiting for me was enough to make me tear up. I bit the tears back. "I'd like prayers for his health."

I was the last one to speak. We fell silent. The radiator began an almost seance-like knocking, and one man said, in a very non-dramatic fashion, "Please hear us." He repeated the prayers everyone had made, and when I heard him say Hodge's name, I felt the lifting of a weight I hadn't been entirely aware of. This was group membership at its best:

now that others knew about Hodge, I didn't have to carry the burden of his illness alone.

When the group broke, there was real fellow feeling. An older woman – the one with the hip problems – took me aside in the hallway.

"I lost a dog two years ago," she said, looking right at me. She had a very gentle face. "I know how hard it can be to have a sick pet."

I couldn't talk, because if I did, I'd cry. I just gave her a brief hug. She smelled like the clementines that had been put out at snack time, and I heard her whisper, "I'll keep Hodge in my prayers."

The next week was entirely different. I walked into the basement with a more expansive attitude. Having connected with the group members, I liked them more. I was relaxed during the meal, and truly appreciative of the leaders' efforts to meet my not-too-demanding vegetarian requests: they'd provided an entirely vegan stew.

I must have looked more positive, because as we were filing out of the basement, one of the leaders – not Tabbi – pointed to a table I'd never really noticed. It was covered with a mix of ordinary books and books published by Alpha.

"If you're interested in learning more," she said, sounding like she was laying the seeds of a conversion, "you might want to read some of these."

It was my most favourite thing: a table covered in books. I was standing in the hall leading to the main doors. All the other participants had shuffled out. I could hear volunteers laughing in the kitchen, but the basement was big, and the kitchen was far away. I had the delicious sense of being on my own as I started to browse.

I skipped past Alpha's *The Holy Spirit* and *Questions of Life* and noticed *What Is the Christian Attitude Towards Homosexuality?* This didn't alarm me. I figured it would be some version of "Hate the sin, love the sinner." And there was some of that, but this booklet went further. There was a children's playroom behind me, and I read leaning against its glass wall. There wasn't a lot of light in the hallway, and I found myself squinting: first just to focus, and then in a sort of stunned disbelief. Homosexuals, the book said, were sinners. AIDS was the inevitable result of that sin. The disease was a judgment from God.

I flipped to the copyright page, desperately trying to get a fix on whether this was an old publication that had just never been culled. The date was 2004. I was swamped by images of AIDS deaths: the emaciation, the abandonment, the open sores, the fear. *God's judgment?*

The words kept circling around in my mind, first in question form, and then as a statement I couldn't get out of my head: AIDS was a judgment from God. Was this what the group really believed? Worse, had I been intentionally steered to the booklet? I suddenly felt like I didn't know the course leaders or anyone associated with the program. There were people I liked, but now I didn't know what they believed, or whether they'd like me if they knew who I was.

It wasn't a great moment. I was shivering, and I realized that a great anger was welling up within me. I felt disgusted, and taken. I knew the others would be in the meeting room, that my absence would be missed. It wasn't that I didn't care; I just couldn't join them. In trying to escape rejection, I'd been rejected once again, this time in a way that had left me feeling brutalized, as slapped around as the pigs in the trucks. *God. Sinner. Judgment.* The words felt wedged inside me, like someone had forced them down my throat. I stood like that for some time, almost ready to throw up, violated, well aware that I couldn't stay.

It's a deep-seated trait of mine to become heavily analytical when I'm most upset. So the day after discovering the Alpha book, I made a list. It was an informed list of possible reactions, based on what I'd read about common responses to rejection.

Response one, according to researchers, is to try to join a different group. But rejection had led me to the porcupine problem, and when I had tried to join two friendly congregations, my spiky bits had kept others at bay.

Response two is to opt out, an idea I had initially dismissed but was starting to see as possibly inevitable.

Response three is to hide or cover the basis of the rejection. In my case, this meant not mentioning I was gay. But this had failed in a rather spectacular fashion, since it had left me alone in a hallway at the Alpha course reading about God's wrath.

Which left option four: join together with other rejected people.

This didn't really appeal to me. Remember when I said I didn't like public school? That was true, but I kind of liked the popularity part. It was the ultimate affirmation of my desire to be accepted, the non-stop social equivalent of someone saying, "Emily? Yeah, she's pretty cool."

Joining with other rejected people flew in the face of my desire to be popular. It was the adult equivalent of hooking up with the unpopular kids outside the drama club doors. Because that's how the gay Catholics struck me: like the kids from school who just never fit in.

I'd known about the gay Catholics all along. They were a secretive group that wasn't very good at keeping secrets. I knew about their services – the way they met upstairs in a downtown church in a room no one needed. There was a second-class status to them that bugged me. Someone had told me that you had to take a side door to get to the unused room, and – boom! – the whole group might as well have been the outcasts from high school, talking about a play no one else cared about.

I sent my initial email with a sense of failed inevitability. This was what things had come to. I watched it bounce from person to person before I got a thumb-typed message providing the deets: weird day, weird time, weird room, side door. No info about what would be happening, or whether there would even be a priest.

"Blessings," the sender wrote, signing off.

It didn't feel like a blessing to me.

I showed up at the weird time (six at night) on the weird day (Saturday) and initially went up the wrong staircase. This was an old set of stairs that ended in a wall. It felt like such a symbol of what I doing – following a path that led nowhere – that I almost left. Instead, I started over, making my way alone through the real church to find a second, more industrial staircase leading up to a warren of rooms.

The gay room surprised me. It was simple, almost stark; there was no ornamentation. The walls were white, and the lights were off. A big bay window at the far end of the room let in the last of the setting sun. There were two candles lit on a makeshift altar that was draped in a plain white cloth. There was a cross between the candles, nothing else. People were seated in plastic chairs set up in a circle, with everyone facing the light.

My foray up the wrong staircase had left me running a bit late. This didn't matter. The greeter – a handsome man with a sexy snake tattoo slithering out from under his sleeve – whispered, "I'm Gary," and told me to sit anywhere. Someone was fiddling with a keyboard, and then a man walked in. I thought he was a member of the congregation, since he was dressed like everyone else. Then he opened a backpack and pulled on a bright white surplice and cream-coloured stole. He kept his boots on, then took his seat at the front of the room. He wasn't standing, like an ordinary priest. Just sitting. The late-day light was flooding in around him, and he looked around the room with a warmth of his own. He seemed delighted to see us. There must have been twenty of us looking back at him. I was still feeling like we were the misfits, the ones who'd be left out.

And he took it all away with one word: "Welcome."

———

That's how every service started, with that word: *Welcome.* Sometimes it was repeated: *Welcome, welcome, welcome.* We were solving the porcupine problem by naming the issue – we'd been rejected – and addressing it. We did this through the services themselves – the gusty singing, the hugs instead of handshakes, the overt signs of devotion – and through the sermons, which talked about outsiders, about how inclusion was only real if it included everyone. The service became a place where the rules of belonging were questioned and held upside down: if an edict from on high said that only certain people could belong, it was an edict that was wrong from the start. At one mass, an old priest began by slamming his cane on the floor and shouting, *"Everyone. Everyone* should feel welcome."

There was a theological element to all of this – Jesus born in a manger, the angels revealing themselves to the poor, *Whatever you do for the least of these,* and all that – but the theology didn't matter as much as what the group was doing, which was standing up to rejection and taking it on. I had walked in expecting to feel ostracized, but I wound up feeling included. And I felt included because I was facing the rejection, not running from it or trying to pass myself off as someone who might be acceptable.

I don't want to make this sound easier than it actually was. Once, a man came in smelling of liquor, as if the simple thought of walking back into church was so intimidating that he had to grease himself with drink. Even the priest, Peter, described our undertaking as "fragile"; he talked openly about the fact that togetherness in a small group could give way to a sense of futility, to a sort of hopelessness about never being let in to the larger one.

But I think it was that very threat of hopelessness that led to the sense of belonging. If we'd been on our own, things really would have been futile. Together, we had each other; in fact, so long as the Vatican refused to change its rules, each other was all we had. This led to a strange, bedrock sort of connection. I'd walk in to be met with hugs; people brought special treats for the after-service social; and the socializing wasn't forced. People were usually in a hurry to catch up with each other, to reconnect after a few weeks away. It was the principles of belonging I'd already learned – shared values, shared caring, shared action – enacted in a beautiful room on a strange evening with the lights turned low and someone fiddling at the piano.

I was dealing with rejection in a religious context, but the principle I landed on could work in any sphere. Bonding in the face of rejection has been the basis of acts of connection that have changed the world: women enduring arrests and hunger strikes to gain the vote; African Americans facing guns and dogs to gain equality; gay men locking hands to gain some measure of respect. I think a lot of people who joined these movements probably got there in the same way I came to the gay Catholics: that is, wishing they didn't have to, that inclusion would just be granted.

But sometimes it's not. The context might be minor or huge. When I was a teenager, a girl named Justine Blainey sued for the right to play hockey with boys. I remember thinking this was silly, and my judgment paled in comparison to the abuse being heaped on her by coaches and hockey stars. But she kept fighting and she won, and in doing so she got women more ice time, better funding, better coaches – she created a whole new way for sporty girls to fit in.

Rejection never feels good. There are many ways of responding to it. Walking away is one of them. But you can also stop walking and turn back around. This is harder, but it might lead to a different sort of belonging, maybe one that's richer than the sort you originally sought. When I walk into the gay Catholic services now, a warmth runs through me from my head to my toes. It's not that there's never any awkwardness or periods of nerves. But I sometimes think there's not enough in the world for us to fight against – or, more accurately, not enough ways for us to come together and take a stand. Standing up to rejection gives you that: in bonding with others to demand inclusion, you wind up creating it. Not just for yourself, but for all the others who are with you, the ones who were left out, but who suddenly have a way in.

CHAPTER SIX

Volunteering

Why What You're Supposed to Do to Belong
Might Not Be as Easy as You Think

IF FAITH WAS SOMETHING I knew I had to explore –
both because of its connection-promoting capabilities and
because of my girlhood memories – I knew I also had to try
volunteering. This was because every time I flipped open a
magazine or listened to a radio show about connection,
someone would invariably recommend it. I saw volunteering as fundamentally different from what I'd done on Pig
Island or at the garden. There had been nothing bureau-
cratic about those activities: no forms to fill out, no training sessions to attend, no weeks spent waiting to hear back
from volunteer coordinators. There had also been no pre-
defined roles, no clear assignments, and no one telling me
precisely what to do.

Volunteering was different. I knew this because I'd already
done a lot of it. You simply can't become an environmental
lawyer without racking up an insane number of hours
writing newsletters, running the environmental law club,
and passing around petitions against the bear hunt. These

activities hadn't led to much belonging, but that didn't matter; they had been goal-oriented, with the goal being to get a job. In retrospect, I can see that this objective locked me in in an effective way: I couldn't quit on a non-profit that I hoped to work for one day. In another way, it meant that I wasn't really volunteering. I was, as one expert puts it, using caring as a vehicle for my own personal success.

That being said, I'd still been in what's known as the "voluntary sector" for a long time. So of all the projects I took on in my quest for belonging, this was one where I knew the ropes. I knew how to cold-call executive directors, show up on time, make myself useful, and generally hang around in an inconspicuous way.

These are useful skills in today's society, because volunteering is the other traditional path to connection that's still going strong. People are still engaged with faith, but the number of people attending services has dipped since the 1950s. Time spent volunteering, on the other hand, seems to be on the rise, especially among Gen-Xers and millennials – the groups most likely to have grown up without ties to unions, great good places, political movements, or nationwide clubs. In a way, volunteering has *become* civic life for younger generations, and for others too. We put so much emphasis on it today: volunteering is required for many high school kids, and anyone who has lost a job, moved to a new town, recently gotten divorced, or otherwise found themselves alone will be steered toward it.

It's hard to avoid the *idea* that we should all volunteer. Whole books are written about how good it is for our psychological and physical well-being; it's prescribed as an instant cure to anyone who's lonely; and it's nearly mandatory for the purposes of job applications and admission to coveted schools. It's almost as if the emphasis on volunteering has to be big, because there are a lot of gaps for it to fill, such as the loss of stable neighbourhoods, the disappearance of local hangouts, and the erosion of long-term jobs.

In fairness, there are some advantages to volunteering as a way of building a bigger and more public life. It's free, for instance, and it's open to people who have no interest in religion, or who are interested but don't feel like putting their sexual orientation or pro-choice views through a religious wringer. But I think there might be more blind faith around volunteering today than there is around religion itself. At least religion encourages you to ask questions and examine first principles. It's hard to walk into a church or synagogue without thinking, *Do I believe? Is there an afterlife? And what is up with suffering?*

Volunteering doesn't promote this sort of examination, even though it's presented in quite sweeping terms. When advocates of volunteering tell us that giving someone what we ourselves are longing for brings unexpected rewards, among them a powerful feeling of connection with others like us, we tend to believe it. With so much else in disarray, we *want* to believe it. And the statement is not technically wrong. Volunteering can lead to a sense of connection and to the range of good feelings often summed up as "helper's high": an endorphin rush, improved mood, increased energy, and enhanced self-esteem. The wrinkle, as I came to learn, is that it's not so easy to find the connection that's supposed to be on offer. It's not even so easy to find a way to give.

I could have tried to serve through my church, but I wanted to separate faith from volunteering. Studies do show that people who are active in congregations are more likely to volunteer. This isn't necessarily because they're acting on religious ideals; often, it's simply because the congregation creates the opportunities: you can sign up for the parish clothing drive, help with the soup kitchen, or drop off sandwiches with the street outreach team. Even though my church offered volunteer opportunities that felt meaningful to me, I didn't want a closed loop. I was already spending a fair bit of time with my church group, and I wanted to see what would happen if I came to volunteering from an ordinary, start-from-scratch position. I also made a rule that I would not use any of my specialized skills to get a volunteer gig. I later relaxed this rule as my search for volunteer work got a bit more harried, but at the outset I told myself I would not pull strings or volunteer with any agencies I'd already worked with.

This did not really eliminate many agencies – just environmental ones that liked to litigate. So I had to assess what I wanted to do. This is a smallish-sounding point that's really rather huge. One of the claims made for volunteering today is that all routes to satisfaction and well-being are created equal. Volunteering at a food bank is supposed to get you to belonging as fast as coaching sports at a community centre or helping out at a hospice. But the sheer number of possible options – you can fundraise, you can sort canned goods, you can serve breakfast at the local school – can make the starting line hard to see. The common wisdom is that we should ask ourselves what we're interested in, but this might not be a good guide to what we should be doing. I love to read, and I've been told countless times that I'd make a great literacy tutor. In fact, I'm pretty sure I'd be an awful literacy tutor. I'm impatient, and if that impatience surfaced as a new reader was struggling with a word, I'd probably end up doing far more harm than good.

So in a way, volunteering isn't so much about what's important to you as it is about what you can practically do. And in this realm, what you can do is defined for you. A central point in the research on volunteering is that the opportunities available to us are created by someone else. This was another thing that for me set volunteering apart from Pig Save, or even the garden. There had been no one really in charge of those undertakings; no one ever gave me a role. I could just show up and do as much or as little as I wanted. This is important because – especially in the case of Pig Save – it meant there were no limits. If I wanted to fall apart on a traffic island in the middle of rush hour, I could go for it.

While I did go on to experience strong feelings during my volunteer project, I never again recovered the rush of raw emotion that I had felt with Pig Save. The Princeton sociologist Robert Wuthnow argues that this limiting of our emotional response is part of what volunteering *does*. As soon as you have a real volunteer role – say, you're a server in a soup kitchen – there are boundaries set up around what you should or should not do. And if things get too intense, you're supposed to get out.

When I really was a server in a soup kitchen years ago, a homeless man with a laptop wanted to show me the novel he was writing. He said it was sci-fi. He also started bringing me gifts – a stolen greeting card, a dolphin charm from a batch that another homeless man was stringing onto necklaces. When I told the volunteer coordinator about this, she told me I should keep my distance.

"You don't want to encourage that sort of thing," she said. "You don't know where it's heading."

I knew what she meant by this: that he might be dangerous, or start to expect more from me, or want me to be his friend outside of the soup kitchen. So I did step back, and I still regret this. For all I know, the guy might have been writing the next *Neuromancer*, and most likely all he wanted was some attention. But my role was to extend a bounded sort of kindness, and so no broader feelings or connection ever came into play.

Having been through the mind-meld at Pig Save, and having struggled with the potential wrath of God at the Alpha course, I was okay with the prospect of toning down my emotions. A carefully defined role felt comfortable. Intensity wasn't my goal here. My goal was to try to create connection by signing up with a legitimate group or agency that would provide me with a limited scope of things to do.

All I had to do was find an agency to take me on. I didn't fully understand how complicated this might be until I tried to reach out to my first agency. Sheer randomness drove me through the thicket of choices. I came home one evening from a gay mass and settled into my armchair beside the stack of old photos I'd never managed to hang. This twinning of *gay* and *old* reminded me of the lesbian and gay archives downtown. I love archives. My dad collected old photographs, and I grew up staring at images of the past and trying to imagine myself in those alternate worlds. I knew the gay archives went further than photos. It collected diaries, banners, albums, books – anything that would create a lineage for what had been a mostly silent and silenced history. I had even applied for a job at the archives after returning from Newfoundland. I didn't get the job, but the fact that I'd applied meant that when I called about volunteering, the woman who returned my call had my resumé in hand.

Her name was Geneva, and she told me that I'd already been assigned to one of the archives' subcommittees. She ran the name of the subcommittee past me – it was long and complex – and then started saying she needed people like me. This should have been a good thing. After all, the first leg of Hagerty's Rule is about being needed. But the need on display here felt less like a welcome and more like badgering. The archives regularly put on exhibits, and Geneva said she was looking for people to review artists' contracts, write fundraising applications, and decide on policy points to guide selection decisions.

I was in my kitchen, feeling surprised at the intensity of the call. I didn't know Geneva; this was the first time we'd spoken. She was talking quickly and not really pausing to let me express my own preferences. The one-way conversation was making me feel cornered, like a teenager facing a boyfriend coming on way too strong.

"You know," I said, trying to cool things off, "that sounds a lot like how I spend my days. A lot of solitary work. I was looking for something more social."

"But with your skills, you could contribute so much. And you could take the job description in any direction you wanted."

Job description? I knew that as companies downsized, volunteers were being asked to fill more substantive roles, but I hadn't been prepared for someone to talk so openly about it.

"Think about how you want to build your resumé," Geneva suggested, making this sound like a really fun thing to do.

I remained silent. Leaving law for writing was the professional equivalent of setting my resumé on fire, but I felt this wasn't what Geneva wanted to hear.

"You know, I'm not sure. I'm kind of . . . I was hoping for something more social," I said again.

"Social," Geneva repeated, as if this really was a job interview and I'd just said I wanted half-time work at full-time pay.

I could feel myself being guilted into saying yes, but I felt I had to stand my ground. A volunteer position writing policy papers sounded about as social as living in a cave.

"Maybe I could help with events?" I asked, sounding unusually timid.

She sighed in frustration, but then relented. "Okay, there's an event coming up in a few weeks. You can help with that."

This felt like a major win on my part, which was itself sort of strange. I probably shouldn't have had to argue for the chance to do something for free.

When I arrived for the event, I was half-expecting some blowback, and I got it. Geneva was wearing heavy-rimmed black eyeglasses, and she looked out at me from these portholes with great disappointment, as if I were a soldier who'd refused to serve at the front.

I wasn't feeling guilty. I was having the fun I'd been looking for. The walls of the archives were covered in old posters and book covers, and I was already in time-travel mode, trying to imagine myself as a 1950s lesbian staring at a twenty-cent paperback with two busty and lipsticked women on the cover. I wanted to see the books themselves, but I had been told that many were stored downstairs, and I couldn't go there right then because I had to help with the event I'd volunteered for.

There wasn't a lot of explanation about what I was doing. I was just told that a photographer would be taking a group picture. My role was to get everyone coming in to sign a waiver. It wasn't clear to me why a photographer needed a waiver for what I was imagining as a simple group shot. The event had been organized over Facebook, and there must have been more details posted there, because the others seemed to possess some information I lacked. After signing their waivers, many just pointed to their backpacks and asked where the bathroom was. I directed them, and once everyone had signed their sheets, I went into the living room where the photo was going to be taken.

The archives were in an old house, and the living room was furnished with old things: a heavy wooden table, wooden bookcases, a thick old carpet. The table was covered with items that looked like they'd been grabbed at random – albums, books, pamphlets. A woman in a black cap was trying to fix a turntable, and she playfully pushed an album my way.

"This is my favourite," she said with a smile.

I looked at it and laughed. The band was called the Three Graces, and the cover featured three women posed naked in a field of grazing horses. I wondered if the image had been Photoshopped, and then I remembered you couldn't Photoshop in 1972. This made me worry about the Three Graces placing themselves so close to horse hooves. I was wondering if they'd made it out of the field unbruised when the woman fixing the player asked if I was going to be in the shoot.

"No," I said. "I'm here as a volunteer." I waved my clipboard as proof.

"You can still be in it," she replied.

I decided to tell her the truth. "I don't like having my picture taken."

Maybe it was from a lifetime of looking at old images, but I didn't want to wind up, fifty years later, as a vanished face in a vintage photo. I also didn't like the growing sense I had of not quite knowing what was going on. Everyone seemed to assume that I knew what was up, and the assumption was so pronounced – with Geneva handing me the stack of waivers, and everyone just strolling in the door with their bags – that it was starting to feel a bit too late to ask why I was there.

"Sabrina is a professional," the woman continued, as if this might make a difference. But I already knew this wasn't just someone snapping pics on her cellphone. The carpet was covered in tape, two cameras on tripods sat at the front of the room, and an enormous light box was casting white light on the wall. If anything, the equipment just reinforced my reluctance to pose: this was going to be a proper photograph, something others paid money for and maybe put in a public place.

I was clearly the only one who felt reluctant. Others were now coming in, and they looked eager. In fact, they were dressed up. The theme seemed to be burlesque; I was seeing a lot of bustiers and tiny skirts. One man with heavily tattooed arms and a sleeveless top was forcing his feet into a pair of size-sixteen stilettos; a woman was sporting a fake moustache, a Rocky tank, and leather pants complete with a package. I was in my usual getup, a look a friend once described as "play-date mom": ponytail, fleecy sweatshirt, jeans, and hiking shoes. I thought I should probably get out of the living room before my coolness factor sank any lower.

As I was heading out, I passed the photographer, who was heading in. She didn't look artsy. If I was play-date mom, Sabrina was suburban office worker. She wore no makeup, had an untrimmed brown bob, and was wearing

an orange blouse over a pair of beige chinos. There seemed
to be a mismatch between Sabrina and the people in the
room: if they were so dressed up and sexy, why was she
looking so nondescript?

I was sitting on the steps in the front hall, waiting to hand
out waivers to any latecomers, so I could hear, but not see,
what was going on in the living room. At first, I wasn't really
paying attention. It was all pleasantries. Sabrina was thanking people for showing up, for signing their forms, and for
going to so much effort with their clothes.

"So, now it's time to get started," she said. Her voice
changed. She began to sound excited. "Grab something
from the table," she instructed, "and start reading aloud."

There was a shuffle as people reached for the books and
magazines, then a cacophony of questions: "Can I read
about blow jobs?" "What about tits?" "Are boobs okay?"

"Yes to blow jobs!" Sabrina shouted. "Yes to tits! Yes to
boobs!" People started reading all at once. I heard someone
say, "'Her hand was as soft as the softest glove,'" but the reading wasn't energetic enough. Sabrina wanted more verve.
She told everyone to stop. She had a question for them.

"Will the carpet match the drapes?"

For a second, I thought she was talking about the carpet
in the living room, and I became even more confused:
was this photo about gay history and rugs? Then I got it –
carpet, drapes. She was talking about her own body hair.

"Will it match?" she repeated, in a high, playful tone.

She wouldn't, would she? I had to look. I heard whoops
and hollers as I made my way down the hall. I peeked my

head in the door and there she was: naked from the waist down, no socks, her orange blouse stopping right above her pubic bone.

"It matches!" someone cried, but I was too gobsmacked to confirm. Sabrina was standing half-naked in a public place and encouraging others to disrobe too.

"Take 'em off!" I heard her call. She was preaching to the converted. I stepped back to the hallway, keeping a few protective feet between me and the living room door. But there were more calls – "Do it!" "You slut!" – and I had to glance back in. What I saw was worse than costumes. A costume means you have something on. Here, for several people, clothes were not on. They were on the table, or on the floor. One woman with fully bared breasts smiled at me as I peeked in the door; I noticed she'd kept her baseball cap on.

I almost ran back to my spot on the staircase. Why hadn't anyone mentioned this? Had someone mentioned it, and I'd just not heard? Unlikely. I'm the sort of person who takes note of things like nudity. I'm the sort of person who steers away from nudity. My heart was racing and I could feel my face turning red, even though I was wearing all my clothes. I paused for a moment of reflection: was this the sort of good physiological shift volunteering was supposed to cue? My physiology was definitely in play. My blood pressure was soaring and I was starting to sweat, but I didn't think these were the sorts of changes the authors of articles like "The Activism Cure" had in mind. That cure was supposed to be about dopamine boosts and improved resilience, about feeling less stressed and more in charge of things.

I'm not sure that *resilient* and *in charge* really captured my mood at that moment. People were now posing while Sabrina – having created the defiant, in-your-face attitude she wanted to capture – worked her camera. I never saw the final result, but in my mind it looks like this: a bunch of people, mostly women, are on their knees in a Victorian living room; they're topless or wearing sexy clothes; all are laughing out loud. I think the photo was meant as a riposte to all the suffocating modesty that attaches to the lesbian past, all those long dresses and starched collars and poems about flowers. It was the sort of thing I might like if I were to glimpse it at a gallery, the sort of thing I might call "audacious." But I wasn't really in a high-art state of mind. I was telling myself to guard the doorway – no one else could walk into this crazy scene – and when I heard Sabrina say, "It's a wrap!" I decided my duty was done.

It was clear, when I got home, that I had to regroup. I'd done a lot of regrouping in my faith and neighbourhood projects, but I had never before had to put "clothing" on the list of things I was looking for. And I still wasn't clear what I was looking for. The gay archives hadn't exactly worked out. I still supported the place and applauded its mission, but I needed some distance from the carpet-and-drapes episode. So I was back to square one: what did I want to do? I looked around my apartment again. Was it going to give me another clue? Actually, it did. I looked at the shrine I'd created to my lost home – I'd added another year's worth of Pride beads, bright red this time – and thought of the visit I'd made to my old neighbourhood.

There had been something bothering me about that trip, aside from the fact that they had torn down my house and replaced it with gigantic buildings. It was that so many of these new buildings were covered in mirrored glass, and I knew the glass was dangerous to birds. Toronto is famous for many things: Drake, the CN Tower, a hockey team that hasn't won the Stanley Cup since the first moon landing. But it's also famous, or infamous, for bird strikes. The city sits on a migration route, but it has sixty- and seventy-storey glass towers at the edge of the lake. Since birds don't understand the notion of glass, they fly right into the reflected sky. The result is over a million bird deaths a year in Toronto alone – a figure that rises with each new glass-clad building that goes up.

I knew about the group that scoured the downtown streets at dawn, trying to save birds that weren't yet dead but simply stunned. This sort of work – collecting injured birds by hand – seemed like giving in the pure, selfless way that books on volunteering tended to describe. It would absolutely require clothing. And it would let me vent some of the anger I felt about the idiocy of mirrored buildings in a city filled with birds. The whole reason I hadn't signed up with the group as part of my caring project was that it required just that – signing up – and I'd been looking then for a more informal commitment.

But now formality was okay. I was expecting an application form. I wasn't expecting an hour-long, in-person orientation session; an emailed orientation kit; a five a.m. wake-up call cancelling that morning's planned training session; and then the actual session, which started at six-thirty one week later at the base of a tower downtown.

This felt like an awful lot of preparation, but I figured it would lead to meaningful work. I started off enthusiastically enough. When I arrived at the appointed hour, there were six of us in the empty bank building lobby. No one was saying much, but perhaps it was too early to expect conversation. And we were all, reasonably enough, waiting for our leader to take over. When Monica finally arrived, she looked like the Hollywood stereotype of the birder she actually was: dishevelled hair, layers of clothing, two nets, a *Birds of North America* field guide, and a bunch of paper bags for us to put the injured birds in.

"You have to make sure you never put yourself in any danger," she said as she led us outside. It was six-thirty in the morning on a Saturday. There was no traffic, and we stood beside the empty street. Monica was talking at a rather hectic pace about a variety of things – about how gulls are a sign that songbirds are around, about a lawsuit the group was planning, about the hazards presented by cobwebs, which can trap the legs of birds like glue. It was a lot of information to take in, and Monica seemed to be skipping over some crucial details, like who the people in the group were and what we might have in common. The fact that none of us had introduced ourselves was beginning to make the event feel awkward. I began to ask a friendly looking guy where he lived, but before he could answer Monica started in again about cobwebs, and he just shrugged his shoulders and smiled.

Suddenly, Monica – who really did know her stuff – stopped her monologue and pointed to what I thought was a leaf on the ground. She leaned down and with extraordinary delicacy lifted it to the inside of her palm.

"A warbler," she announced. "Dead."

The bird's eyes were still vividly bright.

"How do you know?" a woman asked, sounding like she wanted Monica to be wrong.

"Hard to explain." Monica was talking more slowly now. She was paying the bird respect by speaking quietly. "It's just a sense you get. This little guy is gone. And it is a guy." She started describing the differences between male and female warblers as our group passed the bird around. I was last in line, and I got to hold it the longest. It was gorgeous, bright green with black bead-like eyes, and still surprisingly warm. I felt the heat leaving its body and felt the urge to try to save it, and I suddenly understood Monica's relentless pace: if you wanted to save any birds at all, you had to be very focused and move very fast.

"But that meant I didn't talk to anyone," I told Laura the next day. We were in her kitchen. She had a big bay window filled entirely with plants, and she was passing a watering jug over each one. I felt a bit guilty about not wanting to go back to the bird work, but it just felt too lonely.

"It sounds like she probably had no sense that people there had needs that went beyond learning about bird strikes. Which means she's going to wind up with a lot of volunteers just like her – people who are happy to wander around on their own, completely intent on their work."

I was starting to agree when Laura put down her watering jug and leaned against the windowsill. The light made her hair shine. I called it brown and she called it auburn, but either way, it was looking very pretty right then.

"I was at this volunteer art gig with homeless men while you were in Newfoundland, and one of the men became overly touchy with this very young woman, and *I* was the one who intervened. The moderately enlightened man leading the group figured the woman just knew how to be careful. But that's not enough."

It's a point that very few people who write about volunteering recognize: the degree of belonging or connection you might find in a group can depend a lot on who's leading that group.

At the bird strike training, I might have made friends with the guy I'd started a conversation with, but the leader had unintentionally cut us off. Belonging is generally cast as something we're supposed to create, but group leaders have the potential to make that sense of belonging inaccessible. Fortunately, I had Laura to put the situation in context, but other people facing the same situation might feel that it's something *they're* doing wrong – when it's not.

It's not entirely fair, though, to criticize the group leaders. Monica was hired to save birds, and she was great at this. It's our culture that has cast groups like hers as pathways to connection – but creating such an environment requires a skill set that some leaders might not actually possess. And the bird strike group had never held itself out as a connection or friendship opportunity. It held itself out as a chance to walk around downtown and look for stunned birds. It was our *culture* that was laying on the expectation of connection and satisfaction. As I considered this, I realized that I had brought interpersonal needs to an activity that revolved around putting birds in paper bags. My need to belong had nothing to do with this, but the emphasis on volunteering as a pathway to connection was so ingrained in me that the group would have had to actively deny it in order to steer me away.

Some groups do deny it. Savvy non-profit leaders know that their organizations are being asked to shoulder social problems they didn't create and respond to social needs they can't meet. When I once again shifted gears and called the executive director of an agency that as part of its work inspected roadside zoos, the first thing that Glenn, the director, said was, "This isn't social, you know. You're not part of a group." He was warning me off. His role was to protect animals; he made it clear that if I was looking for some sort of bonding experience, I should probably phone someone else.

For some reason, the fact that Glenn recognized the problem made me feel that he'd be a pretty good leader, so I met with him for an hour. He looked exactly as you'd expect the leader of an animal welfare agency to look, with tousled hair, a body firm from years of hiking, fur from an unidentified pet all over his jeans. It struck me, in looking at him, that everyone I'd run into in this challenge looked exactly as they were supposed to: Geneva with her hipster eyeglasses, Monica with her birding nets, and Glenn with his Born Free T-shirt and vegan lunch. It was a bit like walking into a play about belonging, with me bouncing from agency to agency as I searched for a role of my own.

Glenn was more relaxed than I expected a professional animal rights advocate to be. His office was in a converted apartment, and we sat in the kitchen and talked about Beth, who both of us knew, and about some other people we had in common – especially an old boss of mine Glenn had known for years. At the time, this felt like small talk, but in retrospect, it turned out to be quite important.

Glenn said that there were two zoos I might inspect. The first was stuffing wild animals into a barn the size of a suitcase. I looked at a drawing of the zoo, and that alone began to make me feel claustrophobic. The barn was mostly windowless, and the thought of so many animals housed with so little light and air was making me terribly sad.

"What's the other option?" I asked, hoping for something even marginally less distressing.

"There's an aviary we're working with. We've already filed two reports. You just need to see if anything's changed."

This sounded manageable. I lined Laura up for a Saturday outing two weeks later. I needed her both because she could help me navigate the killer stretch of highway between Toronto and the town housing the zoo, and because she knew a lot about birds. Once, in law school, when I was staring at a sparrow twisting in a pool of dirt, she cooed, "Oooh, a dust bath! Feels so good!"

I hadn't known that sparrows took baths, let alone in dust, and I said with real admiration, "You're a birdwatcher."

She considered this before responding, "No, I'm a bird *observer*."

I pitched the aviary trip to Laura as a chance to observe some birds. I warned her that these weren't going to be happy birds, and she said, "It's a roadside zoo inspection. I'm not expecting Bolivia."

It's a good thing she wasn't, because the tropical birds we found were housed in conditions about as far from tropical as you could get. There were giant parrots locked in enclosures with their flight spaces closed, a fat cockatiel shuffling from one stand to the next in a three-square-foot cage, and a big macaw whose wings had been clipped so that it couldn't fly; when we arrived, we were asked if we wanted to see it walked like a dog across the yard.

"Um, no," I said to the guide who'd attached herself to us. The rooms were split with the sound of shrieking birds, and the air was full of dust and probably fecal matter, but the guide seemed cheerful and oddly clued out. All the staff must have known the place was under scrutiny, but none of the critical questions I asked seemed to faze the guide.

When Laura and I stopped outside the cage of a giant white parrot that was bald all the way down his front, I asked what was wrong with him.

The guide offered the sort of wide-open answer that didn't seem to fit the situation. "He's OCD," she said with a laugh. "Like, he can't stop plucking himself. He's really not too bad today. His feathers are just gone off his front. Sometimes, he's as bald as a chicken!"

"Why is he OCD?" The question seemed hopeless, but I felt compelled to ask it.

"Well, we can't let him out, ever, because he's vicious. He won't ride your arm. As soon as you go near him, he bites. So maybe he's too cooped up or something?"

The aviary was loud enough for me to whisper to Laura without our guide overhearing.

"I don't think the people here are very bright," I said.

She shook her head. "I don't know. I don't think it's that they're not smart. I think it's that they lack empathy. And no one here seems to know what they're doing." As if to underscore her point, a heavily tattooed man holding a parrot as big as a baby came up and asked if we wanted to pet it. Laura shook her head and took my elbow to steer me to the doors. "It's amateurs training amateurs, so bad information is just getting passed along."

I paused in front of another display. As though in homage to the places the birds or their ancestors had been taken from, many of the cages were painted with Kiplingesque jungle scenes: swinging vines, palm leaves, full moons against wide-open skies.

"No, really," Laura said, as I tried to stop to look at another bird. "I can't breathe. We have to get out."

The air outside seemed clean and the world seemed mercifully quiet after the calls of the imprisoned birds. Laura was pale, and I worried I'd pushed her over some emotional edge. She said no, it was her lungs. Could we sit in the car for a while?

She sat with the windows open as I pulled out my notebook and jotted down as much as I could. Laura was pretty used to this: our whole friendship began with us sitting in classes and scribbling notes side by side.

"So, do you feel *part* of something?" she asked, with a hint of sarcasm that wasn't quite like her. Maybe she was feeling some distress about being hauled to the House of Birds, after all.

"You know, I do." This puzzled me, and I thought it through. It was hard to explain. "Even though I'm not with the group right now, I feel like the group is in my head."

"Will you keep volunteering for them?"

I couldn't think of a reason why I wouldn't. "I like what they do. I like the guy who runs it. I like the *idea* of them."

She reached for her keys and started the car. "Good enough. But you owe me one."

It turned out that Laura was looking for volunteer opportunities at the same time I was. In fact, so was my friend Andrew, Juliette's husband. This meant that of the four people I knew best in Toronto, two were looking for volunteer gigs: Andrew because he had just moved up from Philly and couldn't yet work, and Laura because she wanted to spend more time doing things that had nothing to do with work. Andrew had wanted to volunteer at an outfit called Second Harvest – Toronto's biggest food redistribution centre – but the centre was too far away.

"And everything else just seems depressing," he added. He was waiting for his immigration papers to come through and had too much time on his hands. "I'm not sure what it is I'm supposed to be helping with."

Laura's problem was a bit different. Since she had a job, she wanted a volunteer commitment that didn't feel like one. "I want to be able to participate, but I don't want to lead," she said. "I do enough of that in my job and I don't have the energy to do it as a volunteer."

I felt that my friends were flagging problems I'd run into – finding that too many volunteer gigs required the same skills and presented the same challenges as work, or not knowing where to start – but I wasn't sure of how to advise them. The connection I'd felt at the bird zoo still didn't wholly make sense to me, and I couldn't figure out how to talk about it in a way that would be useful to others.

So when Laura asked me to come to a special Amnesty event with her, I decided to investigate. Laura hates me using terminology from my research, so I didn't say, *It's individualistic altruism!* even though I really wanted to. Individualistic altruism, or volunteering just once for a specific cause, like a juvenile diabetes walk or a beach cleanup, is on the rise. The interesting thing about this kind of event-specific volunteering is that, while it might let you spend time with friends, it doesn't require you to socialize with anyone you don't know, nor does it create ties to the organization hosting the event. This allows rates of volunteering to climb without leading to any increase in our sense of membership; we might be taking action, but we're not necessarily connecting to new people or larger groups. It's a bit like the online petitions that get passed around today: when you sign them, you're doing something, but it doesn't make you feel particularly linked to anything or anyone else.

Still, I wanted to try individualistic altruism. Maybe it *was* possible to get a sense of connection from a one-off gig. After all, the research on belonging is about volunteering itself, not about your links to the host organization. In theory, a well-managed one-off interaction could translate into the same sense of well-being and contentment that's usually associated with longer-term commitments.

The Amnesty event was about insufficient funding for schools on reserves, and the theme was "Have a Heart." We were there to make cards; Laura and I walked in to find three big tables covered with construction-paper hearts and buckets of crayons and markers. There were about twenty people in the room – all women – with each table housing four to six people, but the place was weirdly quiet. Aside from polite requests to pass pens or glue sticks, no one was talking to each other. When I sat down next to Laura, I automatically dropped my voice to a whisper.

"What's the issue here?" I asked.

Laura started explaining – schools on federal reserves get less money than schools on provincial land – but I was distracted by the atmosphere in the room. We were all there for a common purpose, but there was not much sense of commonality. There were two Amnesty greeters on duty, and they were warmly welcoming newcomers, but these conversations didn't continue after the newcomers sat down.

When a tall, cheerful-looking woman with a young boy came in and sat at our table, it was Laura who said hello.

"Hi," the woman replied, lowering her voice as though in keeping with some unspoken rule. "I saw the event on Facebook."

"Us too."

The woman pointed to her son, who was grabbing at the coloured markers. "I want him to get involved in volunteering. It's so important."

The boy was ignoring her. He was now sniffing at a marker, which made me curious. I thought scented markers had been discontinued. I grabbed a blue one and sniffed it myself: nothing.

Laura paused. We had finished our cards and had been reaching for our coats when the mother had come in. It felt a bit strange to sit there halfway dressed for outdoors. But Laura seemed to feel badly. If we left, the young mother might have no one to talk to.

"Mary?" Laura called. The event leader, a quiet, efficient-looking woman who knew Laura from previous Amnesty events, came over. "Mary, this is—" Laura paused and let the young mother give her name.

"Ellen saw the event on Facebook," Laura explained. "She's brought her son. Maybe you could tell her what needs doing."

"Certainly." Mary sat down. She wasn't unfriendly; no one there was. It was just that no one had bothered with the sort of basic introduction that Laura had just initiated.

"I couldn't just leave her there," Laura said to me as we made our way down the stairs. I remained silent. I wasn't going to criticize Amnesty after having made Laura breathe tropical bird dust. And she didn't seem as put out as I might have expected.

"You never know how these things are going to turn out," she said philosophically. "You do what you can."

"Did that fit your criteria?" I asked.

"What criteria?"

"You know, about participating without having to lead."

"Oh," she said. "That doesn't apply to Amnesty. I've been part of Amnesty so long I don't even think of it as volunteering."

"Wasn't that just a volunteer event?"

"Well, for the others. And sort of for you. But not for me. I'll show up anywhere." She said this cheerfully, as if Amnesty were a troublesome relative whose company she secretly enjoyed.

I did a bit of math. Laura was forty-two, and she'd been volunteering with Amnesty since she was eighteen. That added up to a twenty-four-year commitment, the sort of lifelong tie that people used to bring to groups like the Legion and the Elks. And the commitment itself flowed from her family – her parents were both members – as well as from the faith tradition she'd been raised in. This was probably why she didn't see Amnesty as a deliberate commitment. It wasn't anything she had had to choose or force herself to do. It was just part of her life.

I wondered if the ideas about volunteering as a way of belonging were really about this, about a search for the sorts of lasting connections that people used to have with groups. And this in turn made me wonder if my rule about not contacting any agencies that I had worked for was misplaced. Maybe the key to feeling connected in such a wide-open field really was continuity.

With this in mind, I logged on to the website of an environmental agency I'd volunteered with for two years when I was in law school. The website said that volunteers were a critical part of the group's success and that they welcomed anyone who had an interest in joining. I did as I was told: I sent a brief email saying who I was and what I was interested in, as well as a short message saying that I was happy to do anything, including stuffing envelopes or helping with events. I hit "send" on my message and waited.

There was no response. A few days went by. Then a week. Then one more week. Finally, I processed what had happened: a non-profit agency with a specific call for volunteers hadn't even acknowledged my request to volunteer, let alone responded to it or given me anything to do. I wasn't necessarily expecting a human response, but I didn't even receive an automatic message thanking me for my interest. I felt embarrassed. I'd been involved with that agency for years in the past; my name might have been familiar. Didn't they want me? I knew my note had almost certainly gone to an email account no one checked, and that really it was a computer that was failing to get back to me, but the silence still felt personal.

Maybe it was just that group, I reasoned. So I tried another outfit I'd spent years helping out in the late nineties and early aughts. Their website was different from the previous one, since there was no tab for volunteering. Their main public involvement page was labelled TAKE

ACTION. As soon as I clicked on it, I was presented with the preferred way of taking action: donating money. But doing things *aside* from donating money had become part of my challenge, so I continued to click around. There weren't a lot of meaningful options. I could write to cosmetics companies and ask them to remove chemicals from lipstick, join an annual run and pledge money to the group, sign up for the newsletter, or – if I was really and truly bent on leaving my house – I could volunteer, though this notice was short and vague and made reference to "professional services" I wasn't sure I could offer.

Both organizations seemed to know that they should hold out volunteer opportunities; they didn't want to look like closed shops. But it became clear to me that neither group had any real desire for volunteers. I thought that perhaps this was just the case for the sector I was interested in, but when I followed up on the data, I learned that *half* of public organizations today have no volunteers or public members at all. They're professionally staffed; they don't need outsiders. It's a good stat to keep in mind: roughly 50 per cent of the groups you think might be really great to help out with will likely not need or want you.

Having this spelled out for you – in my case, the first agency did so by simply never returning my email – can leave you feeling even less engaged than you formerly were; it can demotivate you in the search for connection, especially if the organization that rejects you is the only one you've reached out to. Worse, when an organization limits your involvement to seemingly inconsequential activities – such as writing letters to the presidents of cosmetics companies – it can be hard to avoid the message that you're inconsequential too.

So when Glenn from the zoo-monitoring agency got back in touch with a new opportunity, I jumped at the chance to properly "take action." I'd felt good after the trip to the House of Birds, and I had been doing odd tasks for him here and there – a bit of research, a quick memo – but this was a real outing. In fact, it was the sort of thing volunteers live for: a group get-together at an animal sanctuary to discuss problems at a local zoo. I think Glenn, who kept insisting that his group wasn't social, understood quite well that volunteers need some sense of team spirit to keep them going. So he was offering the chance to actually connect – to sit with others, talk, and make decisions that might lead to change.

I was thrilled. I'd never been to an animal sanctuary before. It was north of Toronto, on a big farm tucked behind a thick row of cedars. A nineteenth-century farmhouse sat in the middle of a cheerfully nineteenth-century scene: huge pigs moving placidly in their muddy pen; three dogs racing around; cows grazing lazily, their big eyes lifting toward me without any fear. A guy who I thought was a stable hand but who turned out to be the owner led me to an old barn and, after shooing the dogs away, unlocked a massive wooden door and told me I'd find the horses on the other side. I stepped into the sunlight and absorbed how wonderful everything was: dirt underfoot and fresh air all around. Compared to the misery of the pig trucks, it felt like heaven.

I walked to the edge of the field and held out my hand to the dappled mare a few yards away. I saw Glenn step out of the barn after me, and my pose became a bit more formal. The funny thing about doing volunteer work for animal welfare is that it takes place mostly in offices or on street corners, so you rarely get a chance to actually be *nice* to animals. This was my chance to prove how much I cared. I pretended not to notice Glenn. I stretched out my arm even further, softened my eyes so that I looked transported, and flattened my hand into the horse-friendly position I remembered from my teens: palm open, fingers down. My arm was just above the top rung of a wire fence. I took a step closer.

Glenn was now standing silently beside me, comfortable in his hiking boots. He watched me watch the horse, and then said quietly, "You know, that fence is electrified."

I felt so cheated. "That's not fair!" I yelled, dropping my arm and laughing. "I was so close!"

"It was a very nice try," Glenn said, smiling. "A+ for animal efforts."

Despite my near electrocution, I had a great time at the animal sanctuary. After the meeting, Glenn drove me back to Toronto, and we got to talking about how he had been at this work since I was in high school. He didn't sound like he was boasting. He was just explaining that his commitment to the cause had been lifelong.

When I got home, I thought of how Laura had said roughly the same thing. Her relationship with Amnesty had begun in high school and continued right through undergrad and then law school. In fact, this commitment had guided her life in the same way that Glenn's had guided his: Glenn had become a professional animal welfare activist, and Laura had become a human rights lawyer. (Even though she had left this line of work, she'd still sometimes floor me by saying things like, "You're going to the Gap? Isn't that one of the three major clothing companies that haven't signed the Accord on Fire and Building Safety in Bangladesh?")

This made me wonder if what was missing from the volunteer experience was some sense of a past, or at least of continuity. It's not that we need to lash ourselves to the mast of a single cause and stay there for life. But so many things in our world have become abbreviated – shorter jobs, shorter marriages – that I think we've lost sight of how important continuity can be. I felt like I could easily sign on with Glenn because the work he was doing was an extension of the work I'd done for Beth. Furthermore, the fact that Glenn was friends with an old boss of mine meant that my past and present were linking up. When I had called him up, I hadn't been starting entirely from scratch.

Before I'd begun to explore volunteering, I had made a rule that I wouldn't try to volunteer through faith groups. I'd done this despite having read the research showing that members of congregations are more active volunteers. Now, in the midst of my project, I understood the research more clearly: congregation members were more likely to volunteer because the opportunities being held out to them flowed from a community they were already part of. I'd seen the same sort of rollover effect in my neighbourhood. When I'd gone to a cleanup at a local park, I had met people I knew from the garden. To them, and to me, the cleanup wasn't a new commitment but one that originated in the sense of community we'd already created in the place that we shared.

Considering all this now, it seems to me that the claims for volunteering might be true – it can lead to connection, a sense of service, helper's high, and all the rest – if only we attach one caveat: the work you choose should be related to something you've already done. This approach would have the immediate effect of eliminating the fog of randomness that surrounds volunteering today, and it would also mean that volunteers would be more likely to feel grounded if their commitments started to feel odd or challenging.

I can, for example, imagine a different sort of person having a very different experience at the gay archives. Someone who had worked as an archivist, and who had had years of experience volunteering with LGBT organizations around town, probably wouldn't have been as flummoxed by the nudity that arose. That person would have had a framework in place for making sense of the details; perhaps he or she might even have removed some clothing and joined the shoot.

I'm not sure that volunteering was ever meant to be undertaken in the way that I approached it at the archives – that is, by picking something I was vaguely interested in and then just showing up. Volunteering started with people helping out in their churches and towns and neighbour-hoods; these "volunteers" weren't doing anything outside the borders of their ordinary lives. Today, though, we've cut volunteering off at the roots. I can log on to the Volunteer Toronto website and scroll down a bewildering list of options until I find one that looks right to me – and some of these options are pretty strange, such as "grooming" (it's not clear from the list whether this means people or horses). But if we take this click-and-shrug approach, we're likely to arrive without any previous experience, which in turn can make the activity feel too light, like it's not really anchored in our lives.

It is true that some of the agencies from my past had closed their doors and no longer wanted volunteers, but I solved that problem by applying the same principle that I used throughout this challenge: branch out. Just as I never expected caring to lead me to pigs, I never expected to find myself at a farm animal sanctuary, standing beside some-one I liked and learning how to spot electric fencing.

Ultimately, what I took from this is that good volunteer opportunities are out there, but they're perhaps not as easy to find as the endless encouragement to "just volunteer!" might suggest. Volunteering can lead to connection, but I think it will get us there most readily if we stop seeing it as an easy route and recognize it for what it is: a road with all sorts of twists and turns of its own, one that's easier to fol-low if you've already got your bearings.

CHAPTER SEVEN

Buying

What You Get When You Pay for Belonging,
and What You Don't

IF WE UNDERESTIMATE HOW complex volunteering can be, and if we keep seeing it as a well-marked street leading straight to connection with little effort invested on our part, it's not very likely to deliver the desired result. But perhaps the most significant thing about the claims that are explicitly made for volunteering – namely, that the process is easy and that it will get you to connection really fast – are less and less true of volunteering and more and more true of something else, and that's buying.

Buying may seem like a strange word to use when discussing connection and belonging. Connection, after all, is about a feeling, not about stuff. When I set out on this challenge, I didn't really think of paying for belonging. I've never been a very good consumer; I wear my shoes into the ground and make do with jackets that are not just last season but last century. I'll keep an umbrella until I have to hold it open above my head with my own hands, and there are whole realms of the commercial world that remain foreign to me: I've never bought a car, a stereo, or even a pair of sexy high-heeled boots.

In some ways, I'm just too much my parents' daughter. Even though the Depression ended late in their childhoods, my mom and dad both lived their adult lives as if further financial ruin might be just around the corner. They didn't stuff money in mattresses, but they were frugal, and I inherited this frugality. In fact, I inherited it literally. The photos my dad left me were all taken during the Depression: dust bowl families in dilapidated cars, sockless miners in laceless boots, and little girls wearing feed sacks as dresses. The poverty depicted didn't seem historical to me. Not only was I aware of people in my own city living on next to nothing (though without the burlap dresses), but I've always seen good fortune as just that: chance. When the recession hit in 2008, I wasn't surprised, because some part of me had been expecting it. Some might call this pessimism, but to me it's just realism. Belief in God I have no trouble with, but faith in the market escapes me.

So it wasn't just that I couldn't afford to pay for regular classes at the yoga studio, or for entry into my beloved old neighbourhood of Riverdale. It was that, deep down, paying for something so fundamentally important seemed risky to me. It didn't fit with my basic distrust of money. I knew that if my income tumbled, or if the whole world started to look again like the world in my old photo collection, then my sense of belonging would dry up as fast as Oklahoma in the thirties. And I'm glad I decided to belong for free. I came to realize that the things I did for free were more interesting and way more alive than the things I paid for. There's not much in the commercial world that can offer the sustained high-voltage togetherness I found on Pig Island, or the reassurance I felt while lying half-asleep on a riser in the garden and listening to bees buzz while inhaling the smell of soil.

But I knew, starting out, that the commercial world had to offer *something*, because people with higher incomes consistently report feeling more belonging and less aloneness. A 2005 study from Australia set out the relationship between money and connection quite neatly, with loneliness rates falling as income rose: people earning $300 or less per week were the loneliest, those earning between $400 and $900 per week were less lonely, and those earning more than $1000 per week were the least lonely of all. A Dutch study published in the same year came to the same conclusion and helpfully added some odds: if you were low-income, you were three times more likely to struggle with loneliness than someone with more cash.

One way of explaining these findings is to suggest that a certain sort of person – say, someone who is talented, kind, and smart – will wind up as both rich and included. But stories of people like Dick Fuld – the former CEO of Lehman Brothers who was so anti-social that he kept an elevator on call so that he wouldn't have to talk to anyone – suggest otherwise, and the research backs them up. When psychologists at the University of California, Berkeley, looked at whether the rich possess more of the traits that lead to belonging (kindness, sensitivity, a desire to please), they found that the wealthy struck out on these fronts. The high-income people in the study were more likely to be behaving in self-focused and unethical ways; in one experiment, it was the rich – not the poor – who were caught taking candy from a jar they'd been told was reserved for children.

But if personality traits aren't the answer, something else has to be, because the rich just seem more immune to aloneness than the rest of us. In fact, psychologists have shown that you don't need to actually be rich to feel this immunity: all you need is for someone to hand you a wad of cash and let you hang onto it for a while. An experiment designed by American and Chinese psychologists did exactly this. The researchers told the student participants that the experiment was about dexterity, and then they split the students into two groups. The first group counted eighty one-hundred-dollar bills; the second group counted eighty pieces of paper. After the counting was over, the researchers asked each student to play Cyberball, a computerized game designed to trigger feelings of aloneness. Students log on as players, and researchers determine how often the ball gets passed to them. Leaving a student out of the game, and forcing him or her to watch others play, is a reliable way of cuing short-term feelings of isolation.

After the ball-tossing game was over, the researchers asked each student how often the ball had been passed to him or her. Here, there was no difference between those who had counted money and those who had counted paper. If someone had been left out of the game, that person said so. The real difference lay in the students' responses to being left out. The students who'd counted paper felt rejected, but the students who'd counted money didn't care as much. They knew they'd been rejected; they just didn't *feel* rejected.

Looking at the results, the psychologists, Xinyue Zhou of Sun Yat-Sen University and Kathleen Vohs of the University of Minnesota, concluded that money was acting much like Tylenol had in the social pain/physical pain experiments: it was making rejection hurt less. But unlike Tylenol, the money was also giving the students something. It was serving as a psychological resource they could draw on in the face of isolation.

But what were they drawing? If money is a resource, what can it be used for? One answer is goods. Students knew they could buy things to make them feel more included. In fact, when the psychologists Roy Baumeister and Nathan DeWall looked at what students bought when faced with rejection, the items selected weren't random. Students who'd been made to feel alone either "bought" Rolex watches from an online catalogue, or they bought real T-shirts and wristbands bearing the name of their school at the university tuck shop. The isolated students didn't buy practical items, like notebooks, nor did they buy self-gifts, like chocolate. The goods they wanted were those that symbolized either high social status or membership in a social group.

This is the sort of buying we're accustomed to. The isolated students in Baumeister and DeWall's experiment bought *things* – watches or wristbands or shirts. It's straight-up consumerism: students handed over money and got objects in return. This sort of "buying belonging" can be pretty effective. When I don a University of Toronto tank top, I really do get a boost of togetherness, because I'm indicating my membership in an alma mater that includes cool people like Margaret Atwood and Malcolm Gladwell. The fact that these people don't know me doesn't matter, because my *shirt* suggests there's a connection.

The transfer of money for objects is relatively limited, though, because a T-shirt or even a Rolex can only take you so far in terms of togetherness. The objects you surround yourself with can suggest group membership, but they can't offer you a real group.

If you shell out for an *experience*, on the other hand, you can buy a group. Not an imaginary one – with me right up there with Margaret and Malcolm – but a real one, where you match with other people, share emotions, and (depending on the setting) sit quite close together. This sort of buying is riskier, since it changes how we think about belonging; in a subtle way, it changes how belonging *feels*. But that doesn't mean you can't buy belonging. You can, and that's the real reason the rich feel more connected: when isolation starts to hit, they throw money at the problem. And it works.

I wasn't prepared for how well it would work until I reached out to my first "buying belonging" activity. As I was surfing around online, I realized that there were all sorts of ways I could buy connection. I could pay for an expedition to the Costa Rican cloud forest; sign up for a class that would teach me the difference between single- and blended-malt

Scotch; or register for coaching that promised to provide me with support for creative projects. I lingered on this last site for a while. My friends and family had pretty much heard as much as they wanted to about my book. If I *paid* someone to coach me, on the other hand, the curiosity and encouragement on offer would be limitless – or rather, would be limited only by my ability to pay.

The prospect of not being able to pay brought me back to myself. I decided I didn't want to buy anything resembling a relationship, since I wasn't sure I'd be able to detach from it if my money ran out. So I decided to try to find belonging through classes that were either one-offs or short-term. The notion of classes seemed suitable in another way: I felt there was something I'd been leaving out of this challenge all along, and that was my interest in meditation.

I've been, if I can use this word, a very active meditator. This is partly because my mother started meditating when I was young, so the practice has never seemed unusual to me, and also because I'm high-strung enough to need accessible ways of calming down. I've always had a fondness for medi-tation groups, which in my pre-market experience were vaguely geeky and always rooted in some sort of community. At U of T, I attended meditation evenings through the Buddhist Studies program; before I left for Newfoundland, I took a ten-week course on mindfulness offered by the Artists' Health Centre; and in Newfoundland, I meditated with a small group at an unused baseball clubhouse.

All of these classes had been free, or nearly free. The Health Centre did charge forty dollars, but it also gave me

months of instruction and three Jon Kabat-Zinn CDs – one
of which I'm still using. I've tended to like the people in
these classes. Not only do other meditators share my values (peace, silence), but they tend to be a bit edge-of-the-
ledge, cheerful but looking for ways to tone down.

None of my previous meditation classes had ever promised very much. In fact, the U of T and Newfoundland classes
had been so low profile that I'd had to dig around to realize
they were even there.

Meditation in the commercial world was different: it
offered results. I knew I'd hit on the right class when I
came across a notice that reminded me of the ad I'd seen
for the subdivision – the one that promised to make older,
more neighbourly ways of life new again. The meditation
ad was more fashionable – it featured Sanskrit – but it
was making the same sort of claims. It told me that if I
attended, I'd learn to connect within myself, and that this
sense of connection would provide me with a solid foundation and integration.

It was all on offer: connection, grounding, and integration with an unstated but positive-sounding entity. And at
twenty-five dollars an hour, this was the sort of belonging
I could afford. I called the studio and paid for a class that
very night. I didn't need any lead-up time, the way I had
with caring and faith. There weren't any public or private
obstacles to overcome. All I had to do was read my credit
card number out over the phone, and I was in.

Walking in, I was pretty impressed. I had to take my
shoes off at the entrance to the studio – this seems to be a

feature of the world of commercial belonging – but I was allowed to keep my socks on, so I didn't feel as self-conscious as I had at yoga. Soft-footed, I made my way into the meditation room, which was painted a calming pink with a cream accent wall. The floors were buffed, and the windows were covered with gauzy white curtains that made the light look gentle and diffuse. There were back rests set out, and I immediately thought, *Stuff!* I'd never been to a meditation class where we were all provided with supports for our backs and piles of blankets for under our bums.

The fact that the room was nicer than usual, however, seemed to mean that I should look nicer too. As I went to gather my blankets, I noticed that everyone I passed was in yoga gear. I got the feeling that often sweeps over me in life, the one that makes me think everyone else has gotten a memo that hasn't been sent to me. How did everyone know to wear yoga clothes? And *why* were they wearing them? One answer that came to mind was matching – I knew that looking alike made people feel more alike – but I'd never before been to a meditation class that required a certain look. Here, people were glancing at my jeans and fleecy sweatshirt, but I refused to feel cowed. I felt I was dressed appropriately for meditation, even if I did surreptitiously loosen my belt.

Soon, I was becoming less curious about clothing and more curious about something else. There was a strange silence to the room. I understood that meditation was about not talking, but I'd never before been to a class where the silence began the minute you walked in the door. Here, in a room of twenty people, no one was saying anything. There was some eye contact, and a few friendly smiles, but not a single exchange. The quiet was borderline monastic. I'm not a big talker, so if I'm thinking that a room is too quiet, there's something going wrong in that room.

The quiet was broken only by the appearance of a woman dressed like me. She was going from person to person, asking them about being "on the list." She had a clipboard with her, and a pen. By the time she got to me, I'd overheard enough conversations to understand that "on the list" meant paid up.

"I paid over the phone," I said, before she could even ask the question.

"What's your name?"

I told her, but she couldn't find me on her sheet.

"When did you call?" she asked, sounding concerned, as if I might turn into someone she'd have to deal with.

"This morning."

Her eyes flitted to the top of the sheet.

"Oh, there you are," she said, with some relief. "They had you at the start, not under *W*."

"Sorry," I said, though I wasn't sure why I was apologizing.

"Not your problem," she replied, nicely enough, before asking the woman beside me whether *she* was on the list.

I decided this woman probably wasn't the instructor. This was partly based on the fact that she wasn't in yoga clothes, but beyond that, I figured her role was instrumental: she was talking about money so that the instructor wouldn't have to.

And in fact, once everyone was confirmed as being "on the list," the instructor appeared. She was beautiful. She had long dark hair falling over her shoulders and wore a bright pink yoga tank with spaghetti straps. Her toned legs were in black knee-length leggings, and she had bracelets around both wrists and an anklet above one foot. The bracelets and anklet were covered in chimes, so she didn't walk in so much as introduce her own personal soundtrack.

"Hi," she said easily, as she settled into a perfect cross-legged pose at the front of the class. She had a boxy radio with her and was plugging it into the wall.

"Is everyone comfortable?" she asked. "Do we want the lights on or off?"

The general consensus seemed to be off. She nodded to the person sitting near the switch, and he stood and flicked off the two overhead lights. The room felt more intimate, and instantly more relaxing.

"How are people doing since last week?" she asked. I was attending the second of a multi-class series, though the materials made it clear that you could show up at any time. "Did everyone do their *homework*?" she asked, in a mock-teacher, singsong way.

There was laughter. Most people had not done their homework, which was to meditate for fifteen minutes each day.

"That's all right," she said encouragingly. "We're just getting started."

She handed a stack of papers to the person nearest her and told us to pass them around, each taking one. I realized that we were getting straight to the content of the course, without the introductions I'd been expecting. But there hadn't been any introductions at the yoga studio, either, and I wondered if this was going to be a constant in the commercial world. Not being named left me feeling slightly uncomfortable. I couldn't escape the idea that if my name was irrelevant, then I might be too.

The anonymity didn't seem to trouble our instructor, who – unless she'd gone through a lengthy roll call on the first day – didn't know the names of anyone in the room. She was focusing on the sheet she'd given us, which had Sanskrit words down the left-hand side and English translations on the right. Even though the instructor was doing running translations for us, I found the process confusing, since she was moving so quickly that I couldn't remember what any of the words were supposed to mean.

But the meaning didn't seem to matter. The Sanskrit words were the mantras we'd chant along to. "And if you turn to the mantras," the instructor was saying, "they'll bring you into contact with the happiness that resides within us, because there's a whole *reservoir* of happiness within us."

I stopped trying to figure out the list and started trying to pinpoint why this idea of an internal reservoir sounded so familiar. I knew it was in line with the course's ad, which had been about finding connection within. I'd never thought of connection this way. Early on in this challenge, I created a sub-rule to accompany Hagerty's Rule. Being a word nerd, I used grammar as a guide. Every time I started a connection project, I asked myself what I was connecting *to*. If I couldn't finish the sentence – *I am connecting to my neighbourhood, I am connecting to a faith group* – then I didn't undertake the activity.

Here, if I understood the instructor correctly, I was connecting to myself. And this grammatical peculiarity – in which I served as both subject and object – made me remember where I'd come across the idea of internal happiness before. Early on, when I had been thinking about how to connect, I'd read a self-help book in which the author argued that all isolated people had to do was create a sense of support within their own *heads*. We're all part of something, he insisted, and therefore never alone: "We have emerged from the flow of life on this planet; we are the result of the struggles of millions of other life forms."

At the time, I'd set the advice aside because it seemed bizarre; I was to *imagine* myself as connected? But the leader of the meditation course was saying essentially the same thing: if I wanted to connect, all I had to do was reach within. It's an idea that experts like Robert Bellah have criticized directly, stressing that our own minds can become pretty lonely places if we stay there too long, and that focusing inwards cuts us off from what we need for connection, especially essentials like shared traditions, shared places, and other people.

But there were twenty people in the meditation room ready to connect in this way, so was my rule wrong? I was still grappling with grammar – could a ball throw a ball to itself? – when the instructor turned her radio on. It was another name-that-tune moment. Where had I heard that sound before? It wasn't music she was playing; it sounded more industrial, like a machine. Then I had it: it was the dial tone on an old land line. It was rising and falling in volume, and the familiarity grounded me. It made me think of real people I could really call, and the notion of reaching out reassured me somewhat.

Feeling soothed, my own natural desire to be nice came into play. The chanting was starting, and soon I was chanting along with everyone else. There were only a few men in the room, but their baritone voices began to stand out nicely. The instructor was the loudest of all. She had a good voice and was nearly singing. I wasn't sure what the chants really meant, but this seemed, if anything, helpful. Since my brain couldn't do anything with the unfamiliar words, it threw in the towel and went to wait this out in some distant corner.

"Let go of the mind, drop into the heart," the instructor called above the chanting.

I dropped down into the heart. I was amazed at how good I was starting to feel. The sun was lowering, throwing shadows into the room, and the room itself was perfectly warm. The phone line sounded like music, and the chants were like stones on a pathway, leading me to some place of contentment. I felt glued in, not so much happy as aligned with things. I flagged the idea for later – obediently staying out of my mind and down in my heart – but I realized I'd have to reassess Robert Bellah's argument. Maybe you *could* find connection within.

"Silence," the instructor said. The dial tone disappeared. The chanting stopped. And the sudden quiet made me realize that there had been noises coming in all along: car wheels down below, people talking on the street, a woman laughing. With my eyes closed and the wood floors underneath me, I had the sudden sense of being in a treehouse, perched high above the road with all these good people who were breathing in and out with me.

It felt kind. I felt like I had on my first trip to the yoga studio, when Derek had taken my feet in his hands and lifted me. I was up. I was high. I remembered the literature on oxytocin – the feel-good hormone – and pictured it coursing through my veins.

We were allowed to stay blissed out for a while, just breathing and listening to people talk outside. Then the instructor started to ask questions. Her voice was low and friendly. She seemed genuinely curious about what we'd felt. One woman said she had started to cry. Another said she had felt devotion. Another said she'd suddenly seen the solution to a problem. I had certainly gotten something from the class. The rhythmic chanting had left me feeling less alone than I had felt even two hours earlier. I didn't feel like saying this, though. I figured I didn't have to, since others were likely feeling the same way.

"So, until next week," the instructor said. "That is, if you decide to attend next week."

I understand that spells have to be broken. In fact, I have a lot of experience in coming out of a meditative state and feeling too gluey-mouthed to talk. But this, again, was a different sort of silence. Even after our shared experience, no one was talking. As I stood beside another woman while

232 COUNT ME IN

we waited to stack our blankets, I tried to smile at her, but she didn't catch my eye. I thought about whether this reaction left me feeling less included and decided that right then, it didn't. The feeling of connection was within me; with the exception of the instructor, I didn't need anyone in the class to provide me with it or help create it alongside me. Or if I did need them, it was an anonymous *them* – since I didn't know anyone's names, everyone seemed interchangeable.

This positive feeling lasted until I got home. As I headed toward my bedroom, I started saying the mantras aloud. Hodgie looked up at me, puzzled. He didn't speak Sanskrit, either.

"Those are mantras, Hodge," I explained.

I lay down on the bed and scooped him up beside me. I was still chanting quietly, but the chants weren't working as they had in the class. Suddenly, the foreign words were leaving me feeling a bit alone.

"Do you want to chant, Hodge?"

Hodge got up and jumped down from the bed. No.

The meditation class puzzled me. There were things about it I didn't like – such as the emphasis on anonymity, and the claim that we could find connection within – but I had to admit that it delivered. Even wearing the wrong thing and feeling intellectually critical, I'd wound up feeling connected. The fact that I couldn't recreate the feeling on my own seemed important, but it didn't mean that the feeling hadn't been there in the studio.

If anything, the feeling of connection had materialized more quickly than it had in my Artists' Health course, where we had each introduced ourselves and shared an example of something arts-related that left us stressed. The sense of connection I had taken from those meditation classes had been a slow build: we all had to appear each week, remember names, and talk to each other. Things at the commercial meditation studio had been way more efficient, largely because none of us had seemed to matter very much. We could head straight into group connection because there weren't any individual personalities or problems getting in the way. It was like taking the freeway instead of some pretty side road: you might lose the scenery, but you arrive at your destination much faster.

I was wondering if what I'd hit on had been a fluke, so I decided to compare my meditation studio results to the results I might find through another paying option. I reconsidered yoga, but one of the problems I'd had at the yoga studio – aside from the lightning-strike rejection in the fruit store and the impossible price – was the fact that I just wasn't very good at it. I'm strong and fit, but I'm about as limber as a hydro pole. Juliette is built like me, and similarly inflexible, and she'd solved the problem by doing Pilates.

"It's scalable," she told me one day over the phone. "You don't have to be good at everything all at once. And it's gentler. You're not going to fall over in a Pilates class. You'll probably wind up feeling really good."

I trusted Juliette on many fronts, and I'd heard her talk over the years about how much she liked her Pilates instructor. She didn't talk about this instructor as a friend, but there was always a note of affection in her voice when she said things like, "Barb just *knew* my neck was off this week. That woman is on her game."

She also told me that Pilates was grounding. I wasn't sure whether she was referring to the exercise itself or to regular contact with the group, but she was clear that a class would leave me feeling more even-keeled.

I needed that right then. In some ways, I was in the perfect frame of mind for buying belonging, since my energy levels were lower than they'd been all through this challenge. This was because Hodge was entering what were to be his last weeks. He'd been peeing outside his box for months, but the situation was getting worse. Some days, I'd walk in and the hallway would be flooded, with pee both under and over the plastic sheeting that I'd laid down. He was vomiting up both food and water, and he could no longer make it onto my bed on his own. One afternoon, I heard him crying in the bedroom and walked in to find him staring at the wall, meowing urgently for no reason. When I lifted him up, he struggled as if he didn't know me, so I put him back down and closed the door. I made it to the kitchen before sinking to my knees and starting to cry on the floor.

So the commercial world seemed kind of welcome right then. One reason the market has done such an efficient job of entering our emotional lives is that a lot of us are too wiped out to hold it at bay. If you're stressed or overwhelmed, buying starts to seem like an attractive option – not just for housekeeping and meal preparation, but for dog-walking, dating services, personal coaching, and a sense of inclusion. With Hodge's final illness draining me of moxie, I wasn't in the mood to *work* at belonging. I just wanted someone to hand it to me, like cake on a plate, without me having to do anything but pay.

Pilates seemed like it might deliver on this feeling-for-cash exchange, because when I called the studio, I was greeted like a friend. The clerk seemed genuinely pleased to hear from me, using my first name repeatedly and telling me I'd love the class. When she said I could do Pilates in socks, I said that was good news, because I had "feet issues."

"Not other people's feet," I added, since I didn't want to sound like a fetishist. "Just my own."

There was a pause and then some polite laughter, even though it had not been a funny joke.

"You can keep your socks on, Emily."

She sounded like she would have talked to me all day, and I understood that this was because she had resources – especially time and money – that other leaders, like Beth and Heidi, had to create from scratch. Someone was paying this woman to be nice to me.

I liked it. When I arrived at the studio that evening, she greeted me warmly. Not warmly enough to make her greeting seem fake, but in an even, eager-to-get-to-know-me way. I couldn't remember the last time a stranger had spoken to me like that. Even at the Alpha course, where there'd been some eye toward conversion, the other participants and even the course leaders had been more naturally distant at first. They were friendly, but they hadn't me feel *special* the way this woman was doing, asking if I had any health problems or injuries the instructor should know about.

"My knee," I said, even though I was really thinking about Hodgie's illness. "I hurt it running a few years ago."

"I'll make sure the instructor knows," she replied and then told me that once I'd taken off my shoes, I was free to enter the room.

The space was gorgeous. When I had told an acquaintance which studio I was going to, she'd said, "Posh," and now I saw what she meant. The entire southern wall was nothing but windows, filled from top to bottom with sunlight, while the floors were very dark. There was almost nothing in the room except for some perfectly arranged equipment on racks, and the contrast between the nearly white windows and the nearly black floors made me feel like I was stepping into a photograph, with the flash having just gone off. There was an extremely delicate diffuser hidden somewhere, leaving the air smelling like mint, and fans running in each corner were making a purring sound that blocked out all noise from the street.

The room felt more like a sanctuary than my church did. I could feel my stress levels drop as my feet hit the sunlit floors. *Here*, I thought, *no one is going to be anything but nice to me.*

I was right. A few more women came in, setting their mats on the ground, and while the atmosphere was friendly – with some waves and smiles – no one talked. This was okay. I was starting to see the appeal of *not* talking, or of letting someone else do all the talking and communicating on my behalf.

Which our leader did quite efficiently. Her name was Maria. She was a tall woman with dark hair piled into a high ponytail and a body so perfectly toned that she looked almost bionic. But her manner was far from intense. She was sociable, asking us how we were feeling, and following up with some of the other class members about whether any injuries had acted up. Then she turned to me.

"Your knee, right?"

She knew I was hurting. Or had been hurt. It didn't matter. She was recognizing the fact that I was injured. My knee injury hadn't been major. My ex, Danielle, had told me not to fuss over it, saying that if I just stopped running, I'd be fine. This woman was going further than my own spouse ever had. She seemed *concerned* about my injury.

I nodded, flexing my right knee.

"We'll be careful about that," she said, and I nodded gravely, as if the alternative might be cutting off my leg.

The class began in much the same way that the yoga and meditation classes had. Maria started talking, almost non-stop. We had circular supports under our backs, and she told us to lift our arms up over our heads, then stretch them backwards, then let our shoulder blades drop downwards. I found the moves comforting – lying on a circular support is a really good way of stretching out your chest – and I absolutely loved it when Maria came around and adjusted us. I felt her hand on my upper arm – "You want to feel the lift from *there*," she said – and I wondered if it would be possible to pay her to pat me down some more. Not sexually, but just in that firm, caring way, a way that suggested she was really in tune with what my body was experiencing.

I was enjoying myself. I hadn't forgotten about Hodge, and this wasn't the sort of environment where I could describe the problem, but that didn't matter, because I was getting that connection-related oxytocin boost. I was feeling *good*. In fact, I was feeling so good that, when the class ended, I thanked Maria profusely. This went beyond what my natural desire to be nice normally called for. I was trying really hard to let her know what a difference she'd made, saying, "Thank you *so* much. I had no idea the class was going to be so great." Part of the reason for this was that since she'd done *all* the work, I felt I had to acknowledge this in some way – in fact, in a more overstated way than I would have in an environment where I'd been called on to do some of the work myself.

I could see that there was an imbalance in our efforts, with Maria doing all the work and me just showing up, but I didn't care. Not only did I not have the energy to do much emotional work right then, but I liked how being cared for and attended to was making me feel. I noticed right away, as I set out for my second class – which I'd been looking forward to all week – that I felt zero anxiety. This was unusual. In all of my other projects, setting out a second time usually left me a bit nervous, since it was an open signal to others that, having checked them out, I now wanted to join them. A second visit created the possibility of rejection, and also the possibility that I'd been wrong the first time, that the group might not be what I thought it was.

There was none of this sort of worry with Pilates. So long as I could pay, I couldn't be rejected, and there was no real way for anything to go wrong. No one was going to scream at me for protesting, I wasn't going to prune the raspberry bushes back too far, I wasn't going to have to wander around a bird zoo fearing what I'd see in the next cage. Everything was going to be *great*, and I knew this because I was paying someone to make it great. I could see that this was a bit warped – I gave money and someone else handed me a perfectly crafted emotional experience – but I didn't care. I was spending my days huddled with Hodge on the bed, or trying to get him to eat. I didn't have the resources to put myself on the line. In fact, I wanted a situation where there *was* no line, where all I had to do was show up and have someone take my stress away.

Which Maria repeatedly did in expert fashion. The pre-amble was always the same. The other women and I would smile and acknowledge each other, but not talk. Then Maria would take over, asking questions about pain, about any changes from the week before. About whether the sun was too bright, or the room too warm, or if there was any other way in which we were at all uncomfortable. And then there would be that touch – her hand strong and efficient – a touch I pretended not to notice but secretly craved.

Afterwards, I'd walk home feeling great. I have a lot of experience with exercise – I work out for over an hour every day – and I knew that my good mood and lowered stress levels couldn't be ascribed only to the physical work I had done. I left the Pilates studio in the same state of mind in which I usually left the garden, or mass. I felt part of something, included. It still wasn't clear, when I ran the grammatical rule, what I was connecting *to*, but I didn't care. Fuck grammar. I was feeling good and included at a hard time in my life, and if I was paying for the feeling, who cared about that, either? Belonging is belonging, I told myself; if it was being offered up so easily in market form, maybe this was an *improvement* over having to create it myself.

The only time things went wrong was when I brought my own baggage to the class. One evening, I was running late. I'd had to bring Hodge to the vet – who was just humouring me at this point, and letting me come to my own decision about when I could let go of Hodge – and after I dropped him off at home, the subway broke down, so I basically had to run three stops to get to the studio on time. I was both sad and physically tired when I arrived. While I could try to park the sadness, the fatigue was a bit harder to manage, since the class demanded a reasonably high level of fitness. So I walked in tired, and a bit edgy, and was disappointed to see Maria on a mat, talking to another instructor. I wasn't sure who was teaching whom, since they were both pulling on the same piece of equipment, but it was clear that Maria's attention was on someone else. And this released a completely childish fit of pique: why wasn't Maria paying attention to *me*?

I responded by lying down on my mat, looking at the white ceiling instead of acknowledging her. *Rejection can run both ways, baby*, I thought, before realizing that Maria probably wouldn't care if I rejected her or not. She might like me and see me as a nice person, but she didn't depend on me the way I was starting to depend on her.

This realization just served to make me more irritable. I noticed, during the class, that Maria seemed a bit tired. (Others probably wouldn't have noticed this, but I'd come off a year of assessing group leaders, so I couldn't miss it.) She wasn't walking around as much, not talking as much, not touching us as much as she usually did.

Some unhinged part of me felt like shouting that I wasn't getting my money's worth, though of course I was. Connection and friendliness weren't advertised on the studio's web page. It was just that Maria offered these things, and I'd come to expect them. At the end of the class, after wiping down my mat, I saw her standing in her usual spot – in the hallway between the windows and the door – and I suddenly felt like *punishing* her: if she wasn't going to be extra nice to me, I wasn't going to be extra nice back. I had a vision of myself walking out without thanking her at all, and I realized, with a shock, that I could do this. This was a commercial transaction. I could be as dismissive as I wanted with Maria, and she'd still have to be nice to me. This idea hit me so hard that I actually came to a halt. It struck me as so wrong – that my rudeness could just lead to further friendliness on her part – and the realization of it being wrong snapped me back into a more normal headspace.

"Thanks, Maria," I said, stopping before I made it to the door. "That was a really good class tonight." I was on the brink of apologizing if I'd seemed hostile, but then I realized that the situation didn't require it. My personality had no role in what was unfolding.

But the fact that my personality had no role also meant that my problems had no role. If I had known Maria for a long time, I'm sure I could have gone up to her and told her about Hodge. But that sort of real sharing would only come after months of interaction – months that would tally up to five or six hundred dollars. Maria and I were nowhere near that point yet. And this was a problem, because what I'd really needed that evening was some comfort. I remembered one morning at Pig Island when the sight of the lake had tripped a switch in my head and left me feeling desolate about losing Danielle.

I'd said to Beth that morning, in a pretty neutral way, that I needed some time near the water. She must have seen me drop down to a bench and just sit there, staring out, because after fifteen minutes she came and sat beside me.

"Danielle?" she asked.

I just nodded. Beth stayed with me. We must have sat on the bench for a good ten minutes before I said, "Well, the pigs await," and Beth checked to see if I was really okay before we crossed back to the island.

In class that evening, Maria couldn't have done anything like that, because she didn't know me and because our roles were uneven. I was a client; she was staff. Even if she had picked up on my distress and had wanted to comfort me – and she might have – I'm not sure how she could have offered the comfort. She might have said that she was sorry, and really meant it, but there was no space in the studio for us to step out of our roles and sit side by side in the way that Beth and I had.

This left me missing Beth, but Beth had also left me with memories I could draw on when missing her or the group. Ditto the garden: even though it had closed down after the summer, the benches were still in place, and I often sat there and just remembered how fun and friendly Heidi had been. With Pilates, there was no place I could access, and no public reminders of a private activity. I was doing some of the moves at home in the evenings, and while they left my shoulders stretched out, they didn't provide me with any larger sense of belonging. They were like the mantras at the meditation class: I needed everything else – the group, the room, the instructor – to be in place so that a sense of connection would flow. Furthermore, none of the friendly women in the class were really my friends. No one was unfriendly or rude to me; it was simply that there was always another group coming in as ours left, so the lobby was busy. It was hard to keep track of who was heading out when, let alone offer someone a meaningful goodbye.

So when the inevitable happened, Pilates was not what I turned to. I put Hodge in his carrier on a sunny day in April. I talked to him the whole time we were in the cab, patting him through the half-open bag. As soon as I walked into the clinic, the receptionist, who recognized me, took me into what must have been the euthanasia room, since it was spacious and had a comfortable, padded chair. I immediately went to this chair and lifted Hodge from his bag. I didn't know what to say to him. He was showing more energy than he'd shown for months, even poking around the edges of the chair I was in. I almost called things off – his eyes looked clearer – but then Dr. Ted came in.

"He looks better," I said, not knowing what to do.

Dr. Ted was truly kind. I understood that I was paying him, but the kindness he was offering had nothing to do with the commercial world. He pulled a chair beside mine and looked at Hodge.

"He is looking better. I bet if I measured his adrenalin levels right now, they'd be sky high. But how do you think he'd be tomorrow?"

"Worse," I said, choking. Then I added, "I don't want to do this."

"If you did," Dr. Ted said, "you wouldn't be the sort of person I'd trust."

We sat in silence for a while, watching Hodge.

"So I guess we should do it, then?" I asked. I was praying he'd say no.

He didn't. He said yes. "I'll give him something to help him relax, and you can spend as much time with him as you want. And when you're ready, I'll give him a shot that will put him to sleep. He might shudder, but he won't feel any pain."

I nodded. I was beyond talking.

Dr. Ted pulled out a syringe. It was the first shot, the one meant to make Hodge relax.

"Pick him up," Dr. Ted said gently.

I did, and the injection went in. Hodge didn't seem to feel it at all. I felt his body grow soft. He settled into a circle on my lap. Dr. Ted left us alone. I stroked Hodge's head, trying to memorize as much as I could: how soft his fur was, how he smelled, how the delicate bones near his eyes felt so lovely against my palm. I was crying, harder and harder.

Dr. Ted came back in. He was looking at me in the chair. Hodge was now nearly asleep. In a quiet voice, he asked, "Are you ready?"

Yes. No. Never.

I spent that evening, and the rest of that week, crying. Not just tearing up, but down-on-the-ground, pulling-at-my-hair sort of crying. I felt so lost, and so guilty. I'd killed my own best friend. And the house didn't just feel empty. It felt abandoned. It was my childhood all over again: I'd walk from room to room, expecting to see him, but he was well and truly gone.

After this, I found I didn't want to go back to the commercial world, not back to Pilates or meditation or anything else. Hodge himself hadn't been part of the commercial world – he'd been a cast-off from it, half dead with starvation when I adopted him. And the wealth of what he'd given me made me recognize how little the commercial world was offering. Mantras. Concern about my knee. Things that felt good but didn't take me very far, activities that provided no real support when the chips were down. The real support was coming from real people – from Laura and Juliette, of course, and from my mother, who created a photo album filled with pictures of Hodge, and also from some of my church friends, who emailed to see how I was doing.

"There's a service this Saturday," Gary wrote. "Will you be there?"

I thought of the time set aside for prayers during the service, when we could all offer up something we wanted the group to pray for. I didn't think I'd offer up a prayer for Hodge – not because he wasn't a person, but because his loss felt, if anything, too personal. But mass would be a chance to be with people, to think about hope and sadness, and to get real hugs – not a professional touch but a big bear hug from Gary, who'd let me rest my head against his shoulder and even cry if I wanted to.

"Yes," I wrote back. "I'll be there." And then added what I felt, which was, "Thanks."

CONCLUSION

Count Yourself In

What I Learned about Belonging,
and What You Can Learn Too

MY EXPERIENCE WITH BUYING belonging made me think that we need to start seeing togetherness in the same way that we see our finances. Just as economists recommend having at least three months' worth of savings on hand, I think we all need at least one group that we can easily access in times of need. The need doesn't have to be sweeping, as it was for me after Hodge's death. It can be a lighter but still important need – a need for new friends, for more fun, more lightheartedness, more excitement.

That's what I was looking for when I started this challenge. What I wasn't quite prepared for was how well connection and togetherness would deliver on these fronts. When I set out, I was expecting connection to leave me feeling good, but in a light way. I never expected the mind-meld experience that came over me at Pig Island; the sense of allegiance that I got from walking into my gay Catholic mass; even the wonderful feeling of relaxation and ease that I felt at the garden.

I think we've forgotten how rich and rewarding these experiences can be. Or at least, *I'd* forgotten. I had taken that sense of belonging I'd found in the Arctic years ago and filed it under "the past." Connection seemed like something I used to have, rather than something I could have right now. Even when I set out to challenge myself and see if I could create belonging, I wasn't quite sure I'd succeed. But – and this still sort of amazes me – I *did* succeed. I learned how to create a richer, fuller, more public life. And that means you can too.

That's maybe the first and most significant thing to understand about belonging: that you *can* create it. You need to believe that you can. The fact that so many of us are leading largely private lives doesn't mean that these are the only lives available to us. There's so much more out there: more groups for us to join, more activities to be part of, more people to get to know.

Before you can access this bigger, more public world, however, you have to stop expecting it to look like your private world. When I set out, especially in my search for local belonging, I wanted everyone to be *just like me*. It was an expectation I was carrying over from my private life. I looked like Laura, and talked like Juliette, so I figured the people I met in my belonging project should look and talk like me too. But the people you get to know and befriend more publicly don't *have* to look and talk like you. In fact, if you limit yourself to matching – and I know how good that can feel – you'll wind up cutting off a huge number of connection possibilities, simply because the people involved differ from you.

Opening yourself up to groups and places where everyone's not like you can take some work. I noticed early on at the gay masses, for instance, that I'd sit near people who in some ways resembled me. Maybe it was a response to feeling so rejected by both the Vatican and the Alpha course, but I wanted to be near the guys (and they were mostly guys) who were about my age and who looked like they held jobs like the one I used to have. Then one evening I fell into conversation with a man in his late eighties, and he started telling me stories of what Toronto had been like in the forties; he showed me his navy ring and talked about life during World War ii. These stories opened up whole new worlds for me – Toronto without skyscrapers! – and I would never have heard them or realized how much I liked Richard if I'd kept trying to make my public social world match my private one.

Wanting to match with others was only one of the attitudes that I brought to this project that wound up getting in the way of it. I think we're all going to have aspects of ourselves that limit or at least shape our search for connection. For me, impatience was a big one. If I were a calmer and more patient version of myself, I might have found connection as a cat cuddler, or turned into the literacy tutor I secretly longed to be. But I'm not calm or patient, and this meant that my own personality was, at times, cutting me off from certain ways of getting involved.

That's okay. The trick is to not beat yourself up for certain behaviours or limitations. A search for belonging shouldn't see an introvert try to turn herself into the life of the party; similarly, it shouldn't see people who love parties silently shelving books at the library. The key to belonging is to work with the traits you have. This will ultimately lead to a better sense of belonging and waste less of your time. Accepting that I was a bit of an adrenalin junkie meant that I didn't force myself into a routine of patting cats at the Humane Society; instead, I recognized that this trait made me better suited for facing the shouts and screams on Pig Island. Remember this: whatever makes you a bad candidate for one activity will probably make you a great candidate for a different one.

It's important to respect both your gifts and your limits and find ways of connecting that are right for you. If those ways aren't right, connection either will not materialize or will disappear. I sometimes wonder what would have happened if I'd been able to stay with Pig Save as it embarked on its more political protests. Could I have become the girl in the pig suit standing in a lit-up sow crate? Could I have gone on vocal marches demanding more protections for farm animals? A different sort of person might have found further worlds and even more richness through these activities, but I'm not that person. While it's possible that I'll change in the future, that doesn't affect what I need for connection in the here and now. As soon as costumes appeared at Pig Save, I was effectively out. I could push myself past my comfort zone, but I couldn't turn into a completely new me.

The thing about belonging is that it's not about turning into a new you. I have a vague interest in diet books, which is slightly strange, since I'm skinny. But the books interest me because I see them as social and cultural barometers of how we're thinking today. If I flip through something trendy, like *The Paleo Diet*, I see it advocating a different sort of self. You're not just supposed to emphasize meat and avoid salt; you're supposed to cook in certain ways and hold certain complicated views about the social and metabolic consequences of agriculture. You are, in a sense, supposed to turn yourself into a different sort of person – the Paleo Person, who might not have much in common with the person you were before.

Belonging's not like that. You don't become someone else. If anything, you turn more fully into who you really are. If the first thing I had to learn about connection was that I could create it, the second was that the only way I was going to be able to create it was by being honest about what I needed and valued. I noticed throughout this challenge, for instance, that I wasn't playing any team sports. This struck me as a pretty big omission, since I know that for many people, team sports are a great way into togetherness.

But the one time I tried to find connection through team sports – and this was over a decade before my belonging challenge – the experience led nowhere. I signed up for a women's basketball league, and even though I was wearing the same team shirt as everyone else, I didn't find much in the way of team spirit. I was there because team sports are supposed to be a great bonding opportunity, but I never felt bonded – and that's because deep down, I don't like team sports. This aversion dates back to grade school, when we were all forced to play baseball, and I'd cringe or pretend not to notice when the ball came my way. The basketball league I joined as an adult wasn't a complete write-off since I met my girlfriend there, but in terms of a larger sense of belonging, it took me nowhere, simply because team sports don't matter to me.

I can easily imagine someone with a love of sports writing this book instead of me. This person might begin by signing up with a local baseball team, then maybe start coaching kids, then settle into a Meetup group that catches all the Jays games at a nearby bar. Then his interests might fan out further, and he'd start lobbying for better local sports facilities, and then possibly begin confronting his fear of *not* being able to play sports by volunteering at a rehab clinic, or getting involved with organizations that work with injured soldiers.

This person's project – even though it would look nothing like mine – would ultimately take him to the same place as me, because all of his activities would be rooted in what he cares about. For me, that thing was and always will be the fate of animals and the natural world. For others, it might be children's health, or urban planning, or water purification projects in Africa.

There's no right or wrong way to ground a connection project. Or, it's only wrong if what you're basing it on doesn't mean anything to you. That would be like me deciding to spend a year playing every team sport I could find, to see if maybe *one* of them offered a sense of connection. And I'd have good reason to do so, because team sports are valued in our society. Even I, who can't jump to save my life, know who Kobe Bryant is. If what matters to you is also culturally valued – in the way that sports or music or fashion might be – that's great. It means that you've got a belonging head start, since you don't need to second-guess yourself or try to be someone you're not.

If the things most meaningful to you aren't culturally valued, you're not necessarily facing an uphill battle. What you're facing – right away – is the need to not discount what's important to *you*. In one sense, my valuing of the natural world meant that I was getting some cultural encouragement, since there are large and influential groups in society – like Greenpeace – that share this value with me. Once I started moving into less mainstream activities like Pig Save, however, I started feeling some pushback, and that taught me how tricky it can be to remain true to yourself and to root a belongingness challenge in what you really need.

So one thing you have to do is think about what it is you really care about. A good way to do this is to recall a time when you *have* felt a sense of belonging, and then try to identify what it was that made that time special. As soon as Genevieve said "belonging" to me, I immediately thought of the Arctic, which in turn made me recall my deep love of animals and of "the land," especially huge expanses of space. Other people will go through the same process only to hit on very different subjects. That's fine. The important thing is pinning down what matters to you.

Once you've worked through what it is you care about, you have to ask yourself what you're expecting to happen. There can be different expectations in play. I've already noted the first expectation that I hauled into this challenge – namely, the idea that everyone should be like me. But subtler ideas can surface as well.

Many experts stress, for instance, that in relying so heavily on private ties, we've forgotten how public ties feel. There's an intensity to the private world that's hard to reproduce in other settings. If I'd walked into the community garden expecting to find the same intimacy that I have with Laura, or with my sisters, I would have left disappointed, because no one was offering to interact with me in that way. The public world offers *less* intensity, and we need to stop seeing this absence of intensity as a bad thing. Ray Oldenburg describes "great good places" as a chance for a little time off. It's a blessing we've lost sight of. Just hanging out and not doing much can be every bit as satisfying as sharing secrets with a BFF. Of course, there's nothing wrong with secrets or BFFS. But we can't expect all of our relationships to look like this; if we do, we'll discount others that could end up being very important to us.

Lower-key relationships can offer something just as important as close ties do. The fact that they're not intense means that they don't have to be there for you every second, so there's less pressure on both you and others, as well as more spontaneity. There's also a group aspect to public ties that's critical. When I walked into the gay mass after Hodgie's death, I did cry on Gary's shoulder, but there were also ten other people I could talk to about what had happened. These people could hear the story and offer a more limited sort of support because I wasn't asking them to prop me up. Since I was asking for less, it was easier for them to be there for me. And since being there for me – or for anyone else in the group – wasn't too demanding, the ties in question were easier to maintain. All anyone really had to do was show up. And if you weren't in the mood that night for a lot of chatter, you could head out, because there would always be another evening when you could connect and re-engage.

Public ties mean we can be with people without having to be *on* all the time, and that's a great, stress-relieving thing. It's not all that we need from life – we do need intensity and strong, one-to-one relationships – but we've forgotten how good less intensity can feel. I noticed it as soon as I walked into the yoga studio at the very beginning of this challenge: all I had to do was lie on the ground and I was part of a group. It was soothing and deeply reassuring. This matters more than we think. The fact that the ties we find through public connection are light doesn't mean they aren't strong. In finding ways of being with people that don't depend on sharing or high emotional involvement, you've opened up new social worlds, worlds you can access even if you're tired, or feeling down, or just not in the mood for much social interaction. I once spent an evening at the garden beside a guy who was totally focused on rebuilding the storage shed, and who said nothing to anyone for hours. But I could tell that he was happy and felt part of the group – and he was part of the group. He might have been shy, or just really into carpentry, but the garden offered him a place where he could be with others without having to *talk* all the time.

If we have to check the expectation that the new people we meet should look and act like our closest friends, we also have to check the beliefs or ideas we might be bringing to our relationships with these new people. Right away, I became fascinated by research showing that connection is partly inside our heads, and that certain thoughts might make it difficult to feel connection even when it's there. For me, my home made the problem manifestly clear: it was an awesome place that I just couldn't see as awesome. For others, a block or bias might arise in relation to local place or even volunteering. You might have had bad experiences with these things in the past, which might cause you to head into a new activity thinking, "*Nothing* will work. This is a waste of time."

That's the sort of language you have to be very alert to. If something feels pointless, ask yourself why. Put yourself through the necessary paces. In my case, I started off by talking to a chair and wound up standing alone in a huge condo development. This wasn't a huge amount of fun. In fact, along with the gays-cause-death scene at the Alpha course, it was probably one of the lowest points that I hit in pursuing this challenge. But it was something I had to do in order to recognize the *ideas* that I was bringing to my search for belonging – namely, that there was no safety for me in the concept of place, and that relationships rooted in place might not be safe either.

I agree with experts like Brian Lakey and Clare Cooper Marcus who argue that a big part of the sense of belonging is in our heads. I also agree with the experts who say that we're too quick to dismiss relationships that don't look like close friendships, and that we want our broader social ties to look too much like our private ties. There's an awful lot of weight to these ideas. If you choose to tackle your own connection project thinking that nothing short of close friendship will satisfy you, you will likely be disappointed.

But there's another whole aspect to connection that doesn't have anything to do with our psychology. It's an important thing to be aware of. We live in a world that, in a strange way, discounts itself. If we're unhappy, unemployed, or broke, we're encouraged to see the issue as a personal problem, and we're supposed to solve it by focusing on whatever it is about us that might be causing the problem. But there might not be anything about us that's leaving us unemployed or broke. The problem might be, to use a technical term, structural – meaning that what feels like a personal shortcoming is actually the result of social or economic conditions, circumstances that you won't be able to change no matter how much you might change yourself.

I don't want to sell personal initiative short, but I think it would be both dishonest and unhelpful for me to say that all you need to do to belong is to look within. In ways both big and small, that's just not true. An awful lot of what feels like a personal, private emotion can be created or hindered by larger, more external factors. It helps to be aware of these factors, because if you're not, you can start blaming yourself for a lack of connection when the problem doesn't have anything to do with you.

To take an example: I was kind of stunned when I realized, during my volunteering project, that one in two organizations no longer has any need for volunteers. There's a long story behind this statistic, and it has to do with the professionalization of work that used to be done for free, but the end result was that *half* of the groups I might have joined had shut their doors to volunteers. If I hadn't done the research and been able to spot the larger problem, I might have wound up blaming myself – thinking that there must be something wrong with me or my approach – when the problem actually originated in changes to the organizations themselves.

Numbers are an easy thing to spot, and in the case of volunteering, I benefited from the work of smart researchers who could explain some of the things I was experiencing: for example, Harvard University's Theda Skocpol, who has explored how group membership in our culture has changed over time. Other problems, though, can be harder to identify, and they don't always get written up as cleanly.

I noticed, for instance, that I often felt a sense of inclusion or exclusion right away when I walked into a group. A sense of inclusion was there at the garden and at Pig Save, and really *not* there at the Alpha course. For a while I couldn't figure this out, since all the groups I'd chosen had similar values to mine, and they all operated roughly the same: they expected people like me to show up and try to join a group of strangers for a specific purpose.

It took me some time to notice that in cases where I felt a quick sense of connection, this was often being created by the group leaders. Beth at Pig Save and Heidi at the garden were both really good at extending a welcome, being friendly, and offering me ways to get involved. Tabbi, on the other hand, who led my Alpha course discussion group, was nervous and overwhelmed; she couldn't let anyone in the group relax because she couldn't relax herself. So part of what I was seeing as a personal reaction – *Wow, this group feels really good* – wasn't personal at all. It flowed in a very logical way from the skills and attitudes the group leaders were bringing to their positions. A good group leader made connection feel easy; a less skilled one cut connection off.

There are ways of handling poor group leadership skills. You can start trying to create relationships laterally by reaching out to other group members, for example. But if the leader is talking non-stop or really driving the agenda, this might be hard to do. Another very valid response, though it might sound cold, is to quit attending that group. Tabbi wasn't the reason I left Alpha – that would be the course materials' off-the-charts homophobia – but if I hadn't left for political reasons, I would have had to decide whether I wanted to keep dealing with Tabbi's poor leadership skills. That answer might have been no. Ultimately, the decision is a personal one: someone with a higher tolerance for boredom might have been able to handle Tabbi; they might even have come up with constructive ways of encouraging group debate. But I'm not that person. Now, if I head into a connection opportunity and see poor leadership skills, my tendency is to walk out, since while I'm

willing to do a lot of work, there's a limit to the *sort* of work
I want to be doing.

At the same time, it's not just other people who can get
in the way of finding connection. People are at least visible:
I could walk into Pig Save every week and see how calm
and welcoming Beth was. What took me much longer to
notice, even though I felt its importance on some level
early on, was how much the public spaces around me were
influencing my relationship with connection.

A lot of experts, like Boston College's Juliet Schor, have
noted that in the early 1980s – which was right around the
time that belongingness rates began to drop – we started
shifting from public to private spending. Less and less
money was and is being dedicated to the things we share,
like public transit, public parks, libraries, and community
centres. (My community centre, just by way of example,
has had a letter missing from its sign for years, since its
budget no longer stretches to non-essential repairs.)

It took me a while to realize that some of the successes
that I was seeing as personal – connection at the garden! –
were really the result of my ready access to public goods.
Someone decided decades ago to reserve land for the park;
a bureaucrat at city hall freed up some money for shovels;
and the community centre where we sometimes filled our
watering buckets was built before major spending freezes
came in and was still taxpayer-funded. If these things hadn't
been in place, I couldn't have found connection, because
there wouldn't have been the necessary infrastructure in
place. There might have been green space (and I would

have felt lucky to have it), but community activities *in* that green space would have been much harder to create.

So part of what we see as a private problem – not enough togetherness – is really the result of public decisions. In hindsight, I realize that I was lucky to play out this whole challenge in a city with a decent public transit system. Even though the system sometimes broke down and left me running to get to Pilates on time, in general I could rely on it to get me to the Greenpeace office, to Pig Save, to church. If it weren't for public transit, I would need a car, and if my car were to break down, I'd have fewer ways of connecting – not because of anything I was or wasn't doing, but because I wouldn't have any way of getting to the places that offered connection.

Recognizing how much belonging the public world was creating for me made me more appreciative of it, and more committed to protecting it. And part of protecting public space is using it. That may seem like a strange thing to say: of *course* someone is going to use a park. But they might not use, or might stop using, the community centre or the local library, simply because private alternatives are available. Whether these alternatives are causing or simply responding to the shrinkage of the public realm is a debate someone else can weigh in on, but there are now plenty of private options open to us, some of which have to do with belonging.

I admit that I went into "buying belonging" in something of a bad headspace: Hodge was dying, and I was feeling depleted and possibly more doubtful than I had at any other point during this challenge. But I was (and remain) skeptical of what the private world had to offer. It's not that it didn't offer belonging; it did. But it was a different sort of belonging – one that I couldn't reproduce on my own, and one that, at least in the Pilates studio, turned me into a slightly less sensitive and less communicative version of myself. If I had kept going and had let myself become even more incommunicative and critical, I might have wound up turning into someone who couldn't connect for free – because you do have to be nice to others and talk to them in the non-commercial world. I would, I think, have wound up in a cash-for-connection loop, one in which I relied on someone else to do most of the work while not gaining any of the necessary connection skills myself.

Because I learned that there are certain skills we need to bring to belonging today. When I was still in Newfoundland, I was interested in what the small place I lived in was giving me. In that case, it was gorgeous scenery, access to Danielle's enormous extended family, and groups – like my meditation group – that felt small and manageable because the population was small and manageable. The book I'd been planning to write had been about arriving from a big city and essentially stepping into a sense of community that was already in place.

I think that's what a lot of us want when it comes to belonging. It was certainly what I wanted a lot of the time, especially in relation to home and neighbourhood. I wanted that feeling of being locked in and included to simply be there.

But I'm not sure that you can just walk into a sense of inclusion today. Looking back, I'm not even sure that the town I left – the one I had been planning to write about – was handing me community as neatly as it seemed at the time. It seems to me now that what the beautiful oceanside town was doing was prompting certain behaviours in me that made belonging more accessible and easier to realize.

That's what most small-town fantasies are really about. The key isn't finding some tight-knit small town; rather, it's finding a place that will let you be a better and different version of yourself – someone who says "hi" easily, who knows people of all ages, and who is both trusting and trustworthy.

You don't need a small town to bring these attitudes or behaviours out in you. I created belonging in the third biggest city in North America, and I was able to do so because I learned to *behave* in certain ways. This went beyond reining in certain ideas and learning that I didn't have to match with everyone in sight. It was about understanding how to react in certain situations and mustering the courage to act even in the face of cultural messages suggesting that I shouldn't.

If you set out looking for belonging, for instance, there's a good chance that you'll run into rejection. The rejection might be relatively minor, like the type I faced in the fruit store after my first yoga class. Or it might be big and scripted, preached from pulpits and broadcast on the news. For the first type of rejection, it's helpful to know that Tylenol can help buffer the pain (there's even research suggesting that taking Tylenol *before* you set out to try to join a group might be a good preparatory step). If you don't feel like dealing with the pain, or if the group's not too essential to you, you can walk away and not have to confront rejection in that context again.

If the activity you're trying to join does matter to you, it's important to understand what rejection does to you and how you should best respond. You have to learn that rejection might leave you feeling more hostile or spiky (or porcupine-like). Just being aware of this happening can help put thoughts and behaviours in perspective and maybe ease you down enough to relax and enjoy the new group you're checking out. When I wound up feeling like I had to race away from the friendly people at the United Church, for instance, I should have asked myself why I was refusing to participate. I should also have explored why I walked in wanting connection and walked out feeling like I didn't want to talk to anyone in sight. A bit of context could have helped me understand that I was still responding to the rejection I'd felt at the Catholic chapel – even though no one at the United Church was rejecting me in that way.

But I also had to learn that I could turn around and face the rejection. When I was trying to rejoin Catholicism, there was pretty much every pressure on me to just give up. Catholicism is a very hierarchical religion, and when the fellow at the top – at the time, Pope Benedict – says he doesn't want you, it doesn't leave you much room to manoeuvre. But even in that straitened circumstance, I realized that there were other people facing the same rejection as me, and learning to steer into the rejection and confront it actually led to the sense of belonging I was seeking.

People have been doing this in various important ways for a long, long time. Even my crazy ancestors, who left England and embarked on one of those risky transatlantic journeys that tended to end before land was in sight, were bonding with fellow outcasts.

The image of a person rowing across the Atlantic on his or her own is a very modern one. I sometimes saw such people in St. John's, since it was a popular jumping-off spot, and I'd wonder why they were doing this strange thing. I wondered even more about the media reports accompanying their efforts, with the details about deprivation, solitude, and endurance all cast in a positive light.

Early on in this challenge, I thought about the emphasis we put on endurance today, and about why so much of what we do together is really about pushing our own personal limits. I think all the efforts we make in this regard – the days without speaking, the miles run uphill, the ice baths, the extreme diets – are signs that we feel the need to learn endurance, and what we're preparing to endure is a certain degree of isolation. (In this respect, learning to discount personal distress and go for weeks without talking are useful skills.) I'm not sure any generation before ours has encountered, or been forced to accept, the same level of aloneness as us. Sometimes the aloneness is glamorized (those plucky sailors in their one-man boats) and other times it's deplored (the old woman found dead in her apartment), but either way, it's not challenged. There's not a whole lot in our culture urging us to join together in real, in-person ways. We can tweet, but we're not encouraged to meet.

Which was why the Occupy movement, when it ripped across North America in 2011, felt so electrifying, and why my caring project felt so important. Even though we're not encouraged to join together in public ways, we still can. Doing this – especially if you have an unpopular political goal in sight – is not just frowned upon. The censure goes further than that. Protestors at the University of California, Davis, were famously pepper-sprayed while kneeling on the ground; when I stood on the side of the road in Toronto with my puppy-and-pig sign, people would *scream* that I was an idiot. I really do think that what's being judged here is not the specific cause, but rather the act of joining. We're just not used to it anymore; unless it's a sports team or an indie band, we don't have many models for it.

Midway through this challenge, I decided to attend a Native rights rally aimed at stopping the Keystone XL pipeline. When I told an acquaintance where I was going, she said, "You'd *do* that? You'd go to a protest?" This was after I had spent more than two months standing on Pig Island, where our little gaggle was exposed to the hostility of the outside world with no protections. The rally my acquaintance was referring to was going to be formally organized and police-protected. I couldn't see why she thought it was a big deal. By that point, walking along a downtown street (and not even being asked to hold a sign) was nothing; I could have done it in my sleep.

Then I realized that my nice and well-meaning acquaintance just didn't know how to protest. She wasn't challenging the idea of supporting Native rights. She was saying that she had no experience in gathering with others to present an idea. She was a bit like me at my first Greenpeace meeting: the prospect of joining a group protest in public seemed a little freaky. Standing up with others was something I had to learn to do. It was a skill I had to master, in much the same way I had to learn to read case law and write memos about planning applications. In fact, it was a harder skill to learn, because reading a court case doesn't come with a healthy dose of embarrassment or questions like *Should I be doing this?*

For most of this challenge – maybe the complete first year – I saw the reluctance to join together publicly as a sort of cultural shortcoming. I thought it was a shame that we'd lost the ability to do this, in the same way that I thought the loss of my great-uncle's fiddle was a shame. The loss seemed like one more page from my personal book of nostalgia, one more interesting thing we no longer had. But then a series of events unfolded that made me place the loss of this skill in a slightly different category than the loss of Uncle Charley's fiddle.

Right as this challenge was winding down, there was a whole series of developments that seemed aimed right at me. For starters, the federal government introduced new rules for sow crates, allowing the animals more sociability, more movement, and more light. I thought of the pig crate display Beth had created for Nuit Blanche and the epic, night-long public education campaign that she and the group had embarked on that evening. Pig Save certainly wasn't the only group involved in changing farming

practices, but it was one of them, and these groups, cumu-
latively, were able to raise enough awareness that the federal
government and even private companies like McDonald's
could no longer ignore the problem.

Then, unexpectedly, the abattoir that Pig Save had been
protesting filed for bankruptcy. That abattoir handled a
quarter of all pigs in Ontario. The change doesn't mean that
factory farming is over. Far from it. But it does mean that
the goal of a small group was met. This was possibly for
reasons not having to do with the group – Pig Save did not
control the finances of a major pork processor. But when the
abattoir did close, a lot of people knew what had gone on
there, and there was no major outcry of the sort you usually
hear when an industry closes shop. A lot of people – both
near and far, and including vegetarians, vegans, and
humanely grown types – were more than happy to see it go.

And perhaps most baffling of all, I woke up one morning
to hear a radio announcer saying that Pope Benedict was
resigning. This in itself was strange: A pope was resigning,
the way the CEO of a bank might? But it was true: Pope
Benedict, who'd been so aggressively anti-gay, was on his
way out. And it was only a few months later that his succes-
sor, Pope Francis, said that he wasn't going to judge gay
people. My gay Catholic listserv lit up like a Christmas tree.
Had he really just said that? Was it true? What did it mean?

Pope Francis's words didn't mean that the Catholic
Church was changing its doctrine. But like the changes to
sow crates, they signalled that there had been a shift in
direction, that things weren't quite the way they had been

before. I was thrilled – not just for myself and the other members of my small group, but for all the other gay Catholics who'd never had the nerve to out themselves or to join a group like mine. Things are now easier for a whole lot of us.

What struck me as strange about these developments was that they were political. (Even Pope Francis's statement, which was provided in a religious context, had obvious political undercurrents.) And I'm not a hugely political person. I don't put candidate signs on my lawn or write letters to politicians. My interest in setting out to create belonging was never political; it was always personal. My whole goal was supposed to be about creating a better life for *myself*.

But here's the kicker. In setting out to build a bigger life for myself, I had to join groups, and these groups wound up contributing to political change. And the causes I was involved with were marginal: a group worried about the welfare of pigs, a small group of gay people. Greenpeace, which I didn't join, landed an even bigger prize: Asia Pulp & Paper, the company logging tiger habitat in Indonesia, made a formal commitment to stop. This means that of the three quasi-political groups I either joined or considered joining, all had an impact in the larger world. Their work led to changes that flowed directly from their willingness to protest, stand up to rejection, and demand a different sort of inclusion.

If I extrapolate backwards and imagine myself not joining these groups, and then imagine no one else joining, it's hard to envision these changes taking place. This was one of the things that drove me nuts about the commercial world. I signed up for both meditation and Pilates after Pope Francis had made his big statement, and after the rules around sow crates had been changed. I'd seen the impact that group efforts could have. Then I was told, as part of buying belonging in the commercial world, to focus on myself. To create connection within. This not only broke all my grammatical and intellectual rules, but it left me politically frustrated. I suppose there's an argument to be made that reflection and physical strength give you the resources you need to lobby for change – those Tibetan monks are certainly not lightweights – but the commercial world wasn't encouraging me to become a Tibetan monk. It was encouraging me to find connection within and then go home, without even talking to the people around me.

Which means that, if this is how we think of connection today – or if we're so tired and worn out that it's the only type of connection we're capable of – we're moving into some very dangerous territory. If we don't join groups or clubs or activities, nothing in our going-solo world is going to change. We'll wind up with more of what we have, and what we have is not enough. It's change that brings us together; it's change that opens the door to better relationships with our fellow creatures and with each other. If we lack the skills to join together – skills that involve facing the possibility of rejection and confronting what we see as injustice – these changes will never occur.

I left this challenge convinced of one crucial thing: we've forgotten that different types of interactions have different consequences. In relying strictly on our private ties, in focusing solely on ourselves, or in glamorizing the isolation of a rower a hundred miles off the Grand Banks, we forget that most of the changes in this world were created by groups, and if we let go of the groups, we let go of the possibility for change.

I'm not saying that a belongingness project has to be political. I still think that belonging is about creating a better, richer life for yourself. But in creating it, and in learning how to connect to places and people, we inevitably veer out into more public realms. I think a world that integrates public and private ties is a more satisfying place in which to dwell. It's a world where you can trade endurance for support, novelty, and togetherness, and this feels great.

We've almost forgotten this sort of good feeling, but not quite. After this challenge was finished, and after I'd found connection in a variety of ways, I was biking over a bridge that crosses Yonge Street, Toronto's main thoroughfare. The street below was closed for a marathon, and runners in bright outfits were jogging downhill. A small group of strangers had formed on the bridge, most of whom, like me, probably hadn't realized that the run was on. But once they saw the runners, they stopped to watch the race, clapping and cheering to show their support. The runners, in turn, looked up. Some laughed, many clapped back in response, others shouted, "Come join us!" It was a bright day with a brisk wind, and it was very quiet with the road closed. Everyone – especially the little group on the bridge – seemed particularly happy, almost ebullient, and one reason for

this was that they'd tripped into the sort of public togetherness that's not so easily available to us anymore, but that
feels so good.

I think we all know that it feels good and that we want
more of it. More specifically, I think we're at a tipping point
where we have to decide whether we're going to match that
desire with action. It would be easy not to. We could get by
with private relationships and commercial experiences and
pre-packaged community of the type you might find on a
cruise. But we want more than that. When the circumstances are right – say, that morning on the bridge, or right
after the sort of huge snowstorm that sees neighbours helping neighbours – we plunge right into a different, more
lively sort of togetherness. But then we pull back.

We don't have to pull back. It's possible to join together
in ways that are meaningful to us. The results won't look
like the 1950s. I'm not expecting all the hipster guys downtown to start sporting Shriner hats (though this might, in
fact, be a cool look). I'm not expecting women to spend
hours at PTA meetings. But we can find newer and just as
satisfying ways of reaching beyond our private circles and
connecting with each other. And when we do that, we create a different sort of public world – maybe one that's a bit
more equal and a lot more welcoming.

The thing is, *we* have to do it. No one is going to find
belonging for you. The market's not going to take you
there. But it can be done. There are others out there, either
already looking or ready to look. All you have to do is join
them. In joining, we can do more, feel more, and be more.

It just takes one step – the first one off the sidelines, the one where you stop being okay with so much aloneness and decide that you want something else. A whole project that might start with the words "I'm new here" and take you very far, into places and experiences you didn't expect, but find that you love.

ACKNOWLEDGEMENTS

Count Me In would not have been written without the support and encouragement of my agent, Suzanne Brandreth, who believed in this book when I couldn't and kept me going when I wanted to stop. Huge thanks also to my editor, Lara Hinchberger, whose smart and inspired suggestions made for a cleaner, more readable book.

To Laura, Jessica, Tony, Alex, and Scott – for being such good friends I can barely believe it. To Maura, Wendo, and Ailsa, who I miss in St. John's. And of course to my family, for being there in too many ways for me to count.

And thanks to all the people I met along the course of this journey. I'm glad the book helped me find you. For all the pig savers, and for the gardeners; for the people at church, and the people inspecting zoos; and for everyone who showed up at meetings or orientation sessions or stood chatting with me in a great good place – thank you for making the world feel bigger, warmer, and more alive. This book would not have been possible without you.

SCALES AND QUIZZES

The following scales and quizzes are included so that you can assess yourself on a few of the topics that have been the focus of *Count Me In*. There are no averages scores, and no right or wrong answers. But thinking about the questions can be interesting. I knew, as soon as I saw the Psychological Home Scale, that I *didn't* put a lot of time and effort into making a place my own, and this made me wonder how I might change both myself and my relationship to place.

It's fine to answer each question with a simple "yes" or "no." I found it useful to take the quizzes more than once over the course of my challenge. While my fear of criticism remained stable, my sense of psychological home and neighbourhood community both became much stronger.

Psychological Home Scale

1. I have grown attached to many of the places
   I have lived.
2. I put a lot of time and effort into making a place
   my own.
3. I feel more relaxed when I'm at home.
4. I surround myself with things that highlight my
   personality.
5. I get a sense of security from having a place of
   my own.
6. I add personal touches to the place where I live.
7. I take pride in the place where I live.
8. I work at making a place my own.

© Sandra Sigmon, Stacy Whitcomb, and C.R. Snyder. Used with permission.

Neighbourhood Sense of Community scale

1. I am quite similar to the people who live here.
2. If I feel like talking, I can generally find someone in this neighbourhood to talk to right away.
3. I don't care whether this neighbourhood does well.*
4. People here know they can get help from others in the neighbourhood if they are in trouble.
5. My friends in this neighbourhood are part of my everyday activities.
6. If I am upset about something personal, there is no one in this neighbourhood to whom I can turn.*
7. I have no friends in this neighbourhood on whom I can depend.*
8. If there were a serious problem in this neighbourhood, the people here could get together and solve it.
9. If someone does something good for this neighbourhood, that makes me feel good.
10. If I had an emergency, even people I do not know in this neighbourhood would be willing to help.
11. What's good for this neighbourhood is good for me.

12. Being a member of this neighbourhood is like being a member of a group of friends.
13. We have neighbourhood leaders here that you can trust.
14. There are people in this neighbourhood other than my family who really care about me.

Note: The above quiz includes items (3, 6, and 7) for which a "no" answer would count as positive.

© Jack Nasar and David Julian. Used with permission.

Fear of Criticism Scale

1. It is important to me to be liked and approved of by others.
2. I am uneasy when I cannot tell whether or not someone I've met likes me.
3. I get uncomfortable around a person who does not clearly like me.
4. I censor what I say because I am concerned that the other person may disapprove or disagree.
5. I am concerned that if people knew my faults or weaknesses they would not like me.
6. When I am with other people, I look for signs of whether or not they like being with me.
7. I am more apologetic to others than I need to be.
8. If somebody criticizes my appearance, I feel I am not attractive to other people.
9. I am afraid of hurting other people's feelings.
10. I find it difficult to say "no" to other people.
11. I do things that are not in my best interests in order to please others.

12. If I think somebody may be upset with me, I want to apologize.
13. I feel I have to be nice to other people.
14. I feel uncomfortable being a nonconformist.
15. I get uncomfortable when I am not sure how I am expected to behave in the presence of other people.
16. I am more concerned that people like me than I am about making important achievements.

© Peter Bieling, Aaron Beck, and Gregory Brown. Used with permission.

SELECTED SOURCES

Two books I turned to time and again while writing *Count Me In* were Robert Putnam's *Bowling Alone: The Collapse and Revival of American Community* (New York: Simon and Schuster, 2000) and *Habits of the Heart: Individualism and Commitment in American Life* by Robert Bellah, Richard Madsen, William M. Sullivan, Ann Swidler, and Steven M. Tipton (Berkeley: University of California Press, 1985).

The additional books and articles listed below don't constitute a complete list of sources. Rather, they're the sources I loved reading, or that gave me new insights and ideas as I thought about belonging.

BOOKS

Abrams, Dominic, Michael A. Hogg, and José M.
  Marques, eds. *The Social Psychology of Inclusion and Exclusion* (New York: Psychology Press, 2005).
Altman, Irwin, and Setha M. Low, eds. *Place Attachment* (New York: Plenum Press, 1992).
Burger, Jerry M. *Returning Home: Reconnecting with Our Childhoods* (Lanham, MD: Rowman and Littlefield, 2011).

Canter, David. *The Psychology of Place* (London: Architectural Press, 1977).

Csikszentmihalyi, Mihaly, and Eugene Rochberg-Halton. *The Meaning of Things: Domestic Symbols and the Self* (New York: Cambridge University Press, 1981).

Fischer, Claude S. *Made in America: A Social History of American Culture and Character* (Chicago: University of Chicago Press, 2010).

Gusterson, Hugh, and Catherine Besteman, eds. *The Insecure American: How We Got Here and What We Should Do About It* (Berkeley, CA: University of California Press, 2010).

Hochschild, Arlie Russell. *The Outsourced Self: Intimate Life in Market Times* (New York: Metropolitan Books, 2012).

Kunstler, James Howard. *The Geography of Nowhere: The Rise and Decline of America's Man-Made Landscape* (New York: Simon and Schuster, 1993).

Marcus, Clare Cooper. *House as a Mirror of Self: Exploring the Deeper Meaning of Home* (Berkeley, CA: Conari Press, 1995).

Nouwen, Henri J.M., Donald P. McNeill, and Douglas A. Morrison. *Compassion: A Reflection on the Christian Life* (New York: Image Books, 2005).

Oldenburg, Ray. *The Great Good Place: Cafés, Coffee Shops, Bookstores, Bars, Hair Salons, and Other Hangouts at the Heart of a Community* (New York: Marlowe, 1999).

Sennett, Richard. *Together: The Rituals, Pleasures and Politics of Co-operation* (New Haven, CT: Yale University Press, 2012).

Skocpol, Theda. *Diminished Democracy: From Membership to Management in American Civic Life* (Norman, OK: University of Oklahoma Press, 2003).

Turkle, Sherry. *Alone Together: Why We Expect More from Technology and Less from Each Other* (New York: Basic Books, 2011).

Wachtel, Paul. *The Poverty of Affluence: A Psychological Portrait of the American Way of Life* (New York: Free Press, 1983).

Wuthnow, Robert. *Acts of Compassion: Caring for Others and Helping Ourselves* (Princeton, NJ: Princeton University Press, 1991).

——. *Loose Connections: Joining Together in America's Fragmented Communities* (Cambridge, MA: Harvard University Press, 1998).

ARTICLES AND CHAPTERS IN BOOKS

Baumeister, Roy, Nathan DeWall, Nicole Mead, and Kathleen Vohs. "Social Rejection Can Reduce Pain and Increase Spending: Further Evidence that Money, Pain, and Belongingness are Interrelated." *Psychological Inquiry* 19 (2008): 145–47.

Baumeister, Roy, and Mark Leary. "The Need to Belong: Desire for Interpersonal Attachments as a Fundamental Human Motivation." *Psychological Bulletin* 117, no. 3 (1995): 497–529.

Bieling, Peter, Aaron Beck, and Gregory Brown. "The Sociotropy–Autonomy Scale: Structure and Implications." *Cognitive Therapy and Research* 24, no. 6 (2000): 763–80.

Brashears, Matthew. "Small Networks and High Isolation? A Reexamination of American Discussion Networks." *Social Networks* 33 (2011): 331–41.

Cristoforetti, Antonio, Francesca Gennai, and Giulia Rodeschini. "Home Sweet Home: The Emotional Construction of Places." *Journal of Aging Studies* 25, no. 3 (2011): 225–32.

Eisenberger, Naomi, and Matthew Lieberman. "Why Rejection Hurts: A Common Neural Alarm System for Physical and Social Pain." *Trends in Cognitive Sciences* 8, no. 7 (2004): 294–300.

Fischer, Claude S. "*Bowling Alone*: What's the Score?" *Social Networks* 27 (2005): 155–67.

Fullilove, Mindy Thompson. "Psychiatric Implications of Displacement: Contributions from the Psychology of Place." *American Journal of Psychiatry* 153 (1996): 1516–23.

Gurel-Atay, Eda, Guang-Xin Xie, Johnny Chen, and Lynn Richard Kahle. "Changes in Social Values in the United States: 1976–2007." *Journal of Advertising Research* 50, no. 1 (March 2010): 57–67.

Hagerty, Bonnie, and Kathleen Patusky. "Developing a Measure of Sense of Belonging." *Nursing Research* 44, no. 1 (1995): 9–13.

Hulchanski, David. *The Three Cities within Toronto: Income Polarization among Toronto's Neighbourhoods, 1970–2005* (Toronto: Cities Centre Press, University of Toronto, 2010).

Hummon, David. "Community Attachment." In *Place*

Attachment, edited by Irwin Altman and Setha M. Low, 253–78 (New York: Plenum Press, 1992).

Lakey, Brian, and Patricia B. Cassady. "Cognitive Processes in Perceived Social Support." *Journal of Personality and Social Psychology* 59, no. 2 (1990): 337–43.

Larson, Reed, Mihaly Csikszentmihalyi, and Ronald Graef. "Time Alone in Daily Experience: Loneliness or Renewal?" In *Loneliness: A Sourcebook of Current Theory, Research, and Therapy*, edited by Letitia Anne Peplau and Daniel Perlman, 40–53 (New York: Wiley, 1982).

Lauder, William, Kerry Mummery, and Siobhan Sharkey. "Social Capital, Age and Religiosity in People Who Are Lonely." *Journal of Clinical Nursing* 15 (2006): 334–40.

Leary, Mark. "Affiliation, Acceptance, and Belonging." In *Handbook of Social Psychology*, 5th ed., edited by Susan Fiske, Daniel Gilbert, and Gardner Lindzey, 864–96 (Hoboken, NJ: Wiley, 2010).

Leary, Mark, Kristine Kelly, Catherine Cottrell, and Lisa Schreindorfer. "Construct Validity of the Need to Belong Scale: Mapping the Nomological Network." *Journal of Personality Assessment* 95, no. 6 (2013): 610–24.

Maner, Jon, Nathan DeWall, Roy Baumeister, and Mark Schaller. "Does Social Exclusion Motivate Interpersonal Rejection? Resolving the 'Porcupine Problem,'" *Interpersonal Relationships and Group Processes* 92, no. 1 (2007): 42–45.

Manzo, Lynne. "For Better or Worse: Exploring Multiple Dimensions of Place Meaning." *Journal of Environmental Psychology* 25, no. 1 (2005): 67–86.

Maran, Meredith. "The Activism Cure." In *The Compassionate Instinct: The Science of Human Goodness*, edited by Dacher Keltner, Jason Marsh, and Jeremy Adam Smith, 195-202. (New York: W.W. Norton, 2010).

Masi, Christopher, Hsi-Yuan Chen, Louise Hawkley, and John Cacioppo. "A Meta-Analysis of Interventions to Reduce Loneliness." *Personality and Social Psychology Review* 15, no. 3 (2011): 219–66.

McPherson, Miller, Lynn Smith-Lovin, and Matthew Brashears. "The Ties that Bind Are Fraying." *Contexts* 7, no. 3 (2008): 32–36.

Nasar, Jack, and David Julian. "The Psychological Sense of Community in the Neighborhood." *Journal of the American Planning Association* 61, no. 2 (1995): 178–84.

Piff, Paul, Daniel Stancato, Stéphane Côté, Rodolfo Mendoza-Denton, and Dacher Keltner. "Higher Social Class Predicts Increased Unethical Behavior." *Proceedings of the National Academy of Sciences* 109, no. 11 (2012): 4086–91.

Schor, Juliet. "The New Politics of Consumption." *Boston Review* (Summer 1999): 4–9.

Sigmon, Sandra, Stacy Whitcomb, and C.R. Snyder. "Psychological Home." In *Psychological Sense of Community: Research, Applications, and Implications*, edited by Adrian Fisher, Christopher Sonn, and Brian Bishop, 25–42 (New York: Kluwer Academic/Plenum Publishers, 2002).

Unger, Donald G., and Abraham Wandersman. "The Importance of Neighbors: The Social, Cognitive, and

Affective Components of Neighboring." *American Journal of Community Psychology* 13, no. 2 (1985): 139–69.

Walton, Gregory, Geoffrey Cohen, David Cwir, and Steven Spencer. "Mere Belonging: The Power of Social Connections." *Journal of Personality and Social Psychology* 102, no. 3 (2011): 513–32.

Zhou, Xinyue, Kathleen Vohs, and Roy Baumeister. "The Symbolic Power of Money: Reminders of Money Alter Social Distress and Physical Pain." *Psychological Science* 20, no. 6 (2009): 700–706.